TEACHER'S PET PUBLICATIONS

LITPLAN TEACHER PACK
for
The House on Mango Street
based on the book by
Sandra Cisneros

Written by
Barbara M. Linde, MA Ed.

© 1998 Teacher's Pet Publications
All Rights Reserved

This **LitPlan** for Sandra Cisneros'
The House on Mango Street
has been brought to you by Teacher's Pet Publications, Inc.

Copyright Teacher's Pet Publications 1998
11504 Hammock Point
Berlin MD 21811

Only the student materials in this unit plan (such as worksheets, study questions, and tests) may be reproduced multiple times for use in the purchaser's classroom. No other portion of this unit plan may be reproduced in any way without written consent of Teacher's Pet Publications.

For any additional copyright questions,
contact Teacher's Pet Publications.

www.tpet.com

TABLE OF CONTENTS - *The House on Mango Street*

Introduction	5
Unit Objectives	8
Unit Outline	9
Reading Assignment Sheet	10
Study Questions	13
Study Questions (multiple choice)	21
Vocabulary Worksheets	35
Daily Lessons	45
Writing Assignment 1	48
Writing Evaluation Form	49
Nonfiction Assignment Sheet	50
Oral Reading Evaluation	56
Writing Assignment 2	62
Extra Discussion/Writing Assignments	65
Writing Assignment 3	74
Vocabulary Review Activities	76
Unit Review Activities	77
Unit Tests	83
Unit Resource Materials	113
Vocabulary Resource Materials	131

A FEW NOTES ABOUT THE AUTHOR
SANDRA CISNEROS

CISNEROS, SANDRA (b. 1954) Sandra Cisneros was born in 1954 in Chicago, Illinois. Her father is Mexican and her mother is Mexican-American. She has six brothers. During her childhood, the family moved frequently between Mexico City and Chicago. She recalls a great deal of loneliness from the constant moves as well as from not having a sister. Cisneros was very shy, and spent a great deal of time reading. *The Little House* was her favorite book, because it described the kind of stable family home she longed for.

Cisneros wrote in secret during her elementary school years. By the time she was in high school she was writing poetry and editing the school literary magazine. While in a creative writing class in college in 1974 she began writing seriously, and developing her own unique voice. She received her B. A. in English from Loyola University in Chicago, and her M. A. from the writing program at the University of Iowa. since she was the only minority female in the class, she felt like an outsider. This feeling led her to develop her unique writing style.

The House on Mango Street was her first book, written in 1983. Her other works are:
My Wicked Ways, (1987); "Ghosts and Voices: Writing from Obsession," Americas Review, 15 (Spring 1987): 69-73; "Notes to a Young(er) Writer," Americas Review, 15 (Spring 1987): 74-76; "DO You Know Me? I Wrote The House On Mango Street," Americas Review 15 (Spring 1987): 77-79; *Woman Hollering Creek and Other Stories* (1991) and *Loose Woman: Poems* (1994).

Ms. Cisneros currently lives and writes in San Antonio, Texas

INTRODUCTION

This unit has been designed to develop students' reading, writing, thinking, listening and speaking skills through exercises and activities related to *The House on Mango Street* by Sandra Cisneros. It includes twenty lessons, supported by extra resource materials.

The introductory lesson introduces students to one main theme of the novel, growing up as a minority female, through a KWL activity. Following the introductory activity, students are given an explanation of how the activity relates to the book they are about to read.

The reading assignments are approximately twenty-five pages each; some are a little shorter while others are a little longer. Students have approximately 15 minutes of pre-reading work to do prior to each reading assignment. This pre-reading work involves reviewing the study questions for the assignment and doing some vocabulary work for 6 to 10 vocabulary words they will encounter in their reading.

The study guide questions are fact-based questions; students can find the answers to these questions right in the text. These questions come in two formats: short answer or multiple choice. The best use of these materials is probably to use the short answer version of the questions as study guides for students (since answers will be more complete), and to use the multiple choice version for occasional quizzes. It might be a good idea to make transparencies of your answer keys for the overhead projector.

The vocabulary work is intended to enrich students' vocabularies as well as to aid in the students' understanding of the book. Prior to each reading assignment, students will complete a two-part worksheet for approximately 8 to 10 vocabulary words in the upcoming reading assignment. Part I focuses on students' use of general knowledge and contextual clues by giving the sentence in which the word appears in the text. Students are then to write down what they think the words mean based on the words' usage. Part II gives students dictionary definitions of the words and has them match the words to the correct definitions based on the words' contextual usage. Students should then have an understanding of the words when they meet them in the text.

After each reading assignment, students will go back and formulate answers for the study guide questions. Discussion of these questions serves as a review of the most important events and ideas presented in the reading assignments.

After students complete extra discussion questions, there is a vocabulary review lesson which pulls together all of the separate vocabulary lists for the reading assignments and gives students a review of all of the words they have studied.

Following the reading of the book, two lessons are devoted to the extra discussion questions/writing assignments. These questions focus on interpretation, critical analysis and personal response, employing a variety of thinking skills and adding to the students' understanding of the novel. These questions are done as a group activity. Using the information they have acquired so far through individual work and class discussions, students get together to further examine the text and to brainstorm ideas relating to the themes of the novel.

The group activity is followed by a reports and discussion session in which the groups share their ideas about the book with the entire class; thus, the entire class gets exposed to many different ideas regarding the themes and events of the book.

There are three writing assignments in this unit, each with the purpose of informing, persuading, or having students express personal opinions. The first assignment is to inform: students will read a piece of non-fiction related to *The House on Mango Street* and write a brief report on the piece. The second assignment is to persuade: students will take the role of one character and argue persuasively with another character. The third assignment is to express a personal opinion: students will write a memoir of their own in the style of Sandra Cisneros.

The nonfiction reading assignment for this unit will be done in conjunction with Writing Assignment #1. Students are required to read a piece of nonfiction related in some way to *The House on Mango Street*. After reading their nonfiction pieces, students will fill out a worksheet on which they answer questions regarding facts, interpretation, criticism, and personal opinions. During one class period, students make oral presentations about the nonfiction pieces they have read. This not only exposes all students to a wealth of information, it also gives students the opportunity to practice public speaking.

The review lesson pulls together all of the aspects of the unit. The teacher is given four or five choices of activities or games to use which all serve the same basic function of reviewing all of the information presented in the unit.

The unit tests come in two formats: all multiple choice-matching-true/false or with a mixture of matching, short answer, and composition. As a convenience, two different tests for each format have been included.

There are additional support materials included with this unit. The resource materials sections includes suggestions for an in-class library, crossword and word search puzzles related to the novel, and extra vocabulary worksheets. There is a list of bulletin board ideas which gives the teacher suggestions for bulletin boards to go along with this unit. In addition, there is a list of extra class activities the teacher could choose from to enhance the unit or as a substitution for an exercise the teacher might feel is inappropriate for his/her class. Answer keys are located directly after the reproducible student materials throughout the unit. The student materials may be reproduced for use in the teacher's classroom without infringement of copyrights. No other portion of this unit may be reproduced without the written consent of Teacher's Pet Publications.

UNIT PLAN ADAPTATIONS

Block Schedule

Depending on the length of your class periods, and the frequency with which the class meets, you may wish to choose one of the following options:
- Complete two of the daily lessons in one class period.
- Have students complete all reading and writing activities in class.
- Assign all reading to be completed out of class, and concentrate on the worksheets and discussions in class.
- Assign the projects from Daily Lesson Fifteen at the beginning of the unit, and allow time each day for students to work on them.
- Use some of the Unit and Vocabulary Resource activities during every class.

Gifted & Talented / Advanced Classes
- Emphasize the projects and the extra discussion questions.
- Have students complete all of the writing activities.
- Assign the reading to be completed out of class and focus on the discussions in class.
- Encourage students to develop their own questions.

ESL / ELD
- Assign a partner to help the student read the text aloud.
- Tape record the text and have the student listen and follow along in the text.
- Give the student the study guide worksheets to use as they read.
- Provide pictures and demonstrations to explain difficult vocabulary words and concepts.

UNIT OBJECTIVES *The House on Mango Street*

1. Through reading *The House on Mango Street* students will analyze characters and their situations to better understand the themes of the novel.

2. Students will demonstrate their understanding of the text on four levels: factual, interpretive, critical, and personal.

3. Students will practice reading aloud and silently to improve their skills in each area.

4. Students will enrich their vocabularies and improve their understanding of the novel through the vocabulary lessons prepared for use in conjunction with it.

5. Students will answer questions to demonstrate their knowledge and understanding of the main events and characters in *The House on Mango Street.*

6. Students will practice writing through a variety of writing assignments.

7. The writing assignments in this are geared to several purposes:
    a. To check the students' reading comprehension
    b. To make students think about the ideas presented by the novel
    c. To make students put those ideas into perspective
    d. To encourage critical and logical thinking
    e. To provide the opportunity to practice good grammar and improve students' use of the English language.

8. Students will read aloud, report, and participate in large and small group discussions to improve their public speaking and personal interaction skills.

UNIT OUTLINE - *The House on Mango Street*

1 Introduction Writing Assignment 1	2 PVR House on Mango Street-Laughter	3 Study ?s House-Laughter Mini-Lesson Voice	4 PVR Gil's Furniture-There Was an Old Woman	5 Study ?s Gil's-Old Woman Mini-Lesson Character Dev.
6 PVR Alicia-A Rice Sandwich Oral Reading Evaluation	7 Study ?s Alicia-Rice PVR Chanclas-Born Bad	8 Study ?s Chanclas-Born Bad Mini-Lesson Fig. Lang.	9 Writing Assignment 2	10 Quiz House-Born Bad PVR Elenita-No Speak English
11 Writing Conf. PVR Rafaela-What Sally Said	12 ??s Elenita-Sally PVR The Monkey Garden-Mango Says Goodbye	13 Study ?s Monkey-Mango Extra Discussion Questions	14 Writing Assignment 3	15 Projects
16 Independent Work	17 Nonfiction Presentations	18 Vocabulary Review	19 Unit Review	20 Test

P= Preview Study Questions V=Do Vocabulary Worksheet R=Read

READING ASSIGNMENT SHEET - *House on Mango Street*

Date Assigned	Assignment	Completion Date
	The House On Mango St. - Laughter	
	Gil's Furniture - There Was An Old Woman	
	Alicia Who Sees Mice - A Rice Sandwich	
	Chanclas - Born Bad	
	Elenita, Cards - No Spanish	
	Rafaela Who Drinks Coconut - What Sally Said	
	The Monkey Garden - Mango Says Goodbye	

WRITING ASSIGNMENT LOG - *House on Mango Street*

Date Assigned	Assignment	Completion Date
	Writing Assignment 1	
	Writing Assignment 2	
	Writing Assginment 3	
	Project	

STUDY GUIDE QUESTIONS

SHORT ANSWER STUDY QUESTIONS - *The House on Mango Street*

The House on Mango Street - Laughter

1. Name the members of the narrator's family.
2. How was the house on Mango Street different than the other houses the family had lived in?
3. Describe the house on Mango Street.
4. Why does the narrator say Nenny is not her friend?
5. What does the narrator want to have someday? (Boys & Girls)
6. What is the narrator's name? What does it mean in English and in Spanish? After whom is she named? (My Name)
7. What did Esperanza buy? How did she go about buying it? (Our Good Day)

Gil's Furniture Bought & Sold - There Was an Old Woman

1. What did the girls discover in the furniture store that made Esperanza feel stupid? (Gil's)
2. What is special about the tree in Meme's yard? (Meme Ortiz)
3. What happened when Louie's other cousin visited? (Louie, His Cousin & His Other Cousin)
4. Where is Marin going in a year? Why? (Marin)
5. What matters, according to Marin? (Marin)
6. What scares the people who come into Esperanza's neighborhood? What does Esperanza think of them? (Those Who Don't)
7. What does Esperanza say the Vargas kids don't have? (There Was an Old Woman)

Alicia Who Sees Mice - A Rice Sandwich

1. What does Esperanza say about Alicia? (Alicia Who Sees Mice)
2. What wise thing did Darius say? (Darius & the Clouds)
3. What happened while the girls were looking at the clouds? (And Some More)
4. Where did the girls get the shoes? What did they do with them? (The Family of Little Feet)
5. What happened when Esperanza took the note asking if she could stay for lunch? (A Rice Sandwich)

Mango Street Study Questions Page 2

Chanclas - Born Bad

1. Why doesn't Esperanza want to dance? (Chanclas)
2. How does Esperanza describe her feet? (Chanclas)
3. To what does Esperanza compare her hips? (Hips)
4. What information about hips does Esperanza have? (Hips)
5. Why does Esperanza want to work? (The First Job)
6. What happened to her at her job? (The First Job)
7. What news had Papa received? What does Esperanza do? (Papa . . .)
8. What did the girls do to Aunt Lupe? Why did they do it? What happened to Aunt Lupe that day? What did Esperanza's mother say about it? (Born Bad)

Elenita, Cards, Palm, Water - No Speak English

1. How does Esperanza describe Elenita? (Elenita, Cards ...)
2. Esperanza asked about a house. What was Elenita's response? (Elenita, Cards ...)
3. Who was Geraldo? What happened to him? How did Marin feel about it?
4. What is different about Ruthie? (Edna's Ruthie)
5. What does Esperanza think about Ruthie? (Edna's Ruthie)
6. What do all of the children in the neighborhood disagree on regarding Earl? About what do they agree? (The Earl of Tennessee)
7. Who are Sire and Lois? What did Esperanza notice about Sire? (Sire)
8. What does Esperanza say about the trees? (Four Skinny Trees)
9. What broke Mamacita's heart? (No Speak English)

Rafaela Who Drinks Coconut . . . - What Sally Said

1. Why does Rafaela's husband lock her in the apartment? (Rafaela Who Drinks Coconut ...)
2. What does Rafaela like to drink? (Rafaela ...)
3. According to Esperanza, what does Sally want? (Sally)
4. Describe Minerva's life. (Minerva Write Poems)
5. Why doesn't Esperanza go out with her family on Sundays anymore? (Bums in the Attic)
6. What does Esperanza say she will do when she is older? (Bums in the Attic)
7. What does Esperanza decide about growing up? (Beautiful & Cruel)
8. What does Esperanza's mother say about herself? What does she tell Esperanza? (Smart Cookie)
9. What happened to Sally? (What Sally Said)

Mango Street Short Answer Study Questions Page 3

The Monkey Garden - Mango Says Goodbye Sometimes

1. How did Esperanza feel when Sally went into the garden with the boys? What did she do? (The Monkey Garden)
2. Why does Esperanza think Sally got married? (Linoleum Roses)
3. What does Sally do all day? Why? (Linoleum Roses)
4. What did the three sisters tell Esperanza? (The Three Sisters)
5. How does Esperanza feel about Mango Street? (Alicia & I)
6. How does Esperanza describe the house she wants? (A House of My Own)
7. What does Esperanza say she likes to do? (Mango Says Goodbye)

ANSWER KEY: SHORT ANSWER STUDY QUESTIONS - *House on Mango Street*

The House on Mango Street - Laughter

1. Name the members of the narrator's family.
    Mama, Papa, Carlos, Kiki, Nenny, and the narrator. Carlos and Kiki are the boys. Nenny and the narrator are girls.

2. How was the house on Mango Street different than the other houses the family had lived in?
    It was their own house.

3. Describe the house on Mango Street.
    It is small and red, with small windows. Some of the bricks are crumbling. The front door is hard to open. There is no front yard. There is a small garage in the back. The house has stairs, but only one bedroom and one bathroom.

4. Why does the narrator say Nenny is not her friend?
    The narrator says Nenny is too young to be her friend. They are just sisters. (Boys & Girls)

5. What does the narrator want to have someday? (Boys & Girls)
    She wants to have a best friend.

6. What is the narrator's name? What does it mean in English and in Spanish? After whom is she named? (My Name)
    Her name is Esperanza. In English it means "hope." In Spanish it means "too many letters." She is named after her great-grandmother.

7. What did Esperanza buy? How did she go about buying it? (Our Good Day)
    She gave five dollars to sisters named Rachel and Lucy. They all chipped in and bought a bike.

Gil's Furniture Bought & Sold - There Was an Old Woman

1. What did the girls discover in the furniture store that made Esperanza feel stupid?
    It was a music box. (Gil's Furniture)

2. What is special about the tree in Meme's yard? (Meme Ortiz)
    The kids chose it for their First Annual Tarzan Jumping Contest. Although he won, Meme broke both arms during the contest.

3. What happened when Louie's other cousin visited? (Louie, His Cousin & His Other Cousin)
   The other cousin was driving a Cadillac. He gave all of the neighborhood kids a ride. They were chased by a police car. Louie made them all get out. Then he floored the car, but it crashed. The police led him away in handcuffs.

4. Where is Marin going in a year? Why? (Marin)
   Louie's parents are going to send her back to Puerto Rico because she is too much trouble.

5. What matters, according to Marin? (Marin)
   It matters if the boys see them and they see the boys.

Gil's Furniture Bought & Sold - There Was an Old Woman . . .

6. What scares the people who come into Esperanza's neighborhood? What does Esperanza think of them? (Those Who Don't)
   They think the residents are dangerous. Esperanza thinks they are stupid.

7. What does Esperanza say the Vargas kids don't have? (There Was an Old Woman)
   They don't have respect for living things or themselves.

Alicia Who Sees Mice - A Rice Sandwich

1. What does Esperanza say about Alicia? (Alicia Who Sees Mice)
   She is a good girl. She studies because she wants a better life. Alicia isn't afraid of anything except mice and her father.

2. What wise thing did Darius say? (Darius & the Clouds)
   He said one of the clouds was God.

3. What happened while the girls were looking at the clouds? (And Some More)
   They started naming the clouds, then began insulting each other's mothers.

4. Where did the girls get the shoes? What did they do with them? (The Family of Little Feet)
   A woman in the neighborhood gave them the shoes. They played in them for awhile, then take them off. Lucy hides them under a bushel basket on the back porch.

5. What happened when Esperanza took the note asking if she could stay for lunch? (A Rice Sandwich)
   The nun said she could only stay that day. She cried in the canteen and ate her greasy, cold sandwich.

Chanclas - Born Bad

1. Why doesn't Esperanza want to dance? (Chanclas)
    She is embarrassed because she is wearing her old saddle shoes with her new dress.

2. How does Esperanza describe her feet? (Chanclas)
    She says they are big and heavy like plungers.

3. To what does Esperanza compare her hips? (Hips)
    She compares them to a new Buick with keys in the ignition.

4. What information about hips does Esperanza have? (Hips)
    She says hips are scientific. The hip bones reveal whether the bones belong to a man or a woman.

5. Why does Esperanza want to work? (The First Job)
    She needs the money for tuition for the Catholic high school.

6. What happened to her at her job? (The First Job)
    An older Oriental man grabbed her face and kissed her.

7. What news had Papa received? How does he reach? What does Esperanza do? (Papa . .)
    His mother had died. He begins to cry, and Esperanza holds him.

8. What did the girls do to Aunt Lupe? Why did they do it? What happened to aunt Lupe that day? What did Esperanza's mother say about it? (Born Bad)
    The girls pretended to be like Aunt Lupe. They mimicked her laugh, walk, and speech. She died the day they were making fun of her. Esperanza's mother said she was born on an evil day and would go to hell.

Elenita, Cards, Palm, Water - No Speak English

1. How does Esperanza describe Elenita? (Elenita, Cards ...)
    She is a witch woman.

2. Esperanza asked about a house. What was Elenita's response? (Elenita, Cards ...)
    She said "Ah, yes, a home in the heart. I see a home in the heart."

3. Who was Geraldo? What happened to him? How did Marin feel about it?
    Geraldo was a young man whom Marin met at a dance. He was in a hit and run accident and died. Marin cannot explain why his death mattered to her.

4. What is different about Ruthie? (Edna's Ruthie)
    She is the only adult who likes to play.

5. What does Esperanza think about Ruthie? (Edna's Ruthie)
    She thinks Ruthie could have been a lot of things if she had wanted to.

6. What do all of the children in the neighborhood disagree on regarding Earl? About what do they agree? (The Earl of Tennessee)
    They don't agree about what his wife looks like. They do agree that when the two of them go into his apartment he holds her by the arm and they don't stay long.

7. Who are Sire and Lois? What did Esperanza notice about Sire? (Sire)
    Sire is a boy in the neighborhood. Lois is his girlfriend. Once Esperanza noticed that Sire was looking at her.

8. What does Esperanza say about the trees? (Four Skinny Trees)
    She says the trees are the only ones who understand her.

9. What broke Mamacita's heart? (No Speak English)
    Her baby boy started singing the Pepsi commercial in English.

Rafaela Who Drinks Coconut . . . - What Sally Said

1. Why does Rafaela's husband lock her in the apartment? (Rafaela Who Drinks Coconut ...)
    He thinks she will run away because she is so beautiful.

2. What does Rafaela like to drink? (Rafaela ...)
    She likes to drink coconut and papaya juices.

3. According to Esperanza, what does Sally want? (Sally)
    She wants to love and love and love.

4. Describe Minerva's life. (Minerva Write Poems)
    She is young, but is married and has two children. She writes poetry at night. She has put her husband out, but he comes back. It appears that her husband beats her.

5. Why doesn't Esperanza go out with her family on Sundays anymore? (Bums in the Attic)
   She is ashamed of the way they stare out the window at things they can't have.

6. What does Esperanza say she will do when she is older? (Bums in the Attic)
   She will own a house and invite the bums in to live in the attic.

7. What does Esperanza decide about growing up? (Beautiful & Cruel)
   She says she will not grow up tame. She has begun her own war. She is leaving the table like a man.

8. What does Esperanza's mother say about herself? What does she tell Esperanza (Smart Cookie)
   She says she used to be smart. She quit school because she did not have nice clothes. She tells Esperanza she has to take care all her own.

9. What happened to Sally? (What Sally Said)
   Her father caught her talking to a boy and beat her.

The Monkey Garden - Mango Says Goodbye Sometimes

1. How did Esperanza feel when Sally went into the garden with the boys? What did she do? (The Monkey Garden)
   She felt angry. She ran to Tito's apartment and told Tito's mother. Tito's mother was not concerned. Then Esperanza went to rescue Sally. Sally did not want to be rescued.

2. Why does Esperanza think Sally got married? (Linoleum Roses)
   Esperanza thinks Sally got married to escape.

3. What does Sally do all day? Why? (Linoleum Roses)
   She sits and looks out the window and at her possessions.

4. What did the three sisters tell Esperanza? (The Three Sisters)
   They told her to remember to come back.

5. How does Esperanza feel about Mango Street? (Alicia & I)
   She says she doesn't belong. She never wants to come from Mango Street.

6. How does Esperanza describe the house she wants? (A House of My Own)
   It is a house of her own. It has a porch and purple petunias. It would be quiet and clean.

7. What does Esperanza say she likes to do? (Mango Says Goodbye ...)
   She likes to tell stories.

MULTIPLE CHOICE QUIZ QUESTIONS - *House on Mango Street*

The House on Mango Street - Laughter

____1. Name the members of the narrator's family. (The House on Mango Street)
       A Mama, Papa, Abuela, Kiki, and the narrator.
       B Mama, Papa, Carlos, Kiki, Nenny, and the narrator.
       C Mama, Papa, Carlos, Mariana, Nenny, and the narrator.
       D Mama, Uncle Lucho, Kiki, Nenny, and the narrator.

____2. How was the house on Mango street different than the other houses the family had lived in? (The House on Mango Street)
       A It was the largest house they had ever lived in.
       B The government was paying for it.
       C It was their own house.
       D It was the first two-story house they had lived in.

____3. Which sentence does **not** describe the house on Mango Street?
       A It is large and blue.
       B Some of the bricks are crumbling.
       C There is no front yard.
       D There is one bedroom and one bathroom.

____4. True or False: The narrator says Nenny is her best friend. (The House on Mango Street)
       A True
       B False

____5. What does the narrator want to have someday? (Boys & Girls)
       A She wants to have a husband and five children.
       B She wants to have a bedroom of her own.
       C She wants to have a best friend.
       D She wants to have a college education.

____6. What is the narrator's name? What does it mean in English and Spanish? (My Name)
       A It is Blanca. In English it means "white." In Spanish it means "pure."
       B It is Esmerelda. It means "shining jewel" in both languages.
       C It is Dolores. It means "sorrowful" in both languages.
       D It is Esperanza. In English it means "hope." In Spanish it means "too many letters."

____7. What did Esperanza buy? How did she go about buying it? (Our Good Day)
       A She chipped in with sisters named Rachel and Lucy. They all bought a bike.
       B She and her sister bought a fancy doll house with furniture.
       C She bought makeup from a friend who sold Avon.
       D She and her brothers bought a new dress for their mother.

Mango Street Multiple Choice Quiz Questions Page 2

<u>Gil's Furniture Bought & Sold - There Was an Old Woman</u>

____1. What did the girls discover in the furniture store that made Esperanza feel stupid? (Gil's Furniture)

        A It was a full-length mirror.
        B It was a book in Spanish, and she could not read it.
        C It was a music box.
        D It was a television. She had never seen one.

____2. What is special about the tree in Meme's yard? (Meme Ortiz)

        A The kids chose it for their First Annual Tarzan Jumping Contest.
        B The kids all built a treehouse in it.
        C It is the first tree Esperanza was ever able to climb.
        D It is the only tree on the street.

____3. What happened when Louie's other cousin visited? (Louie . . .)

        A He tried to sell drugs to them.
        B He gave the kids a ride in a stolen car and was arrested.
        C He took them to see their first movie.
        D Esperanza got a crush on him.

____4. Where is Marin going in a year? (Marin)

        A She is going away to college because she got a scholarship.
        B She is going to live with another aunt in California.
        C She is going to a convent.
        D She is going back to Puerto Rico. She is too much trouble for Louie's parents.

____5. What matters, according to Marin? (Marin)

        A Having good skin and nice clothes matters.
        B Having lots of money matters.
        C It matters if the boys see them and they see the boys.
        D Being loved matters.

____6. True or False: People who come into Esperanza's neighborhood think the residents are dangerous.

        A True
        B False

____7. What does Esperanza say the Vargas kids don't have? (There Was an Old Woman)

        A They don't have any manners.
        B They don't have respect for living things or themselves.
        C They don't have any common sense.
        D They don't have any money.

Mango Street Multiple Choice Quiz Questions Page 3

Alicia Who Sees Mice - A Rice Sandwich

____1. Which statement about Alicia is **false**? (Alicia Who Sees Mice)
    A She is a good girl.
    B She studies because she wants a better life.
    C She is afraid of mice and her father
    D She is much smarter that Esperanza.

____2. What wise thing did Darius say? (Darius & the Clouds)
    A He said one of the clouds was God.
    B He said the clouds looked like angels.
    C He said people and clouds were both beautiful.
    D He said clouds and people change all of the time.

____3. What happened while the girls were looking at the clouds? (And Some More)
    A They all agreed to stay friends for life.
    B They all saw the same animal shapes.
    C They started naming the clouds then began insulting each other's mothers.
    D It began to rain and they all got wet.

____4. What did the woman give the girls? (The Family of Little Feet)
    A jewelry
    B shoes
    C money
    D a china tea set

____5. What happened when Esperanza took the note asking if she could stay for lunch? (A Rice Sandwich)
    A The nun sent her to the nurse. The nurse sent her to the hospital.
    B The nun said no and sent her home.
    C The nun said she could only stay that day. She cried in the canteen and ate her greasy, cold sandwich.
    D The other kids made fun of her sandwich and she ran home crying.

Mango Street Multiple Choice Quiz Questions Page 4

<u>Chanclas - Born Bad</u>

____1. Why doesn't Esperanza want to dance? (Chanclas)
    A Her mother said it is a sin and she is not allowed to dance.
    B She does not know how.
    C She is embarrassed because she is wearing her old saddle shoes with her new dress.
    D She thinks the others will make fun of her.

____2. How does Esperanza describe her feet? (Chanclas)
    A She says they are big and heavy like plungers.
    B She says they are small and dainty like Cinderella's.
    C She says they are her best feature.
    D She says they are ugly and look like banana boats.

____3. True or False: Esperanza compare her hips to a locomotive. (Hips)
    A True
    B False

____4. What "scientific" information about hips does Esperanza have? (Hips)
    A The length of the hip bone can tell how long a person will live.
    B They tell how many children a woman will have.
    C A girl's hips stop growing when she is fourteen.
    D The hip bones reveal whether the bones belong to a man or a woman.

____5. Why does Esperanza want to work? (The First Job)
    A She wants to save and buy a house for her family.
    B She wants to buy new clothes.
    C She needs the money for tuition for the Catholic high school.
    D She is planning to move out when she graduates from high school.

____6. What happened to her at her job? (The First Job)
    A An older Oriental man grabbed her face and kissed her.
    B She got fired for giving a customer the wrong change.
    C She got hurt and was sent home.
    D She was late because she took the wrong bus.

____7. What news had Papa received? How does he react? What does Esperanza do? (Papa . .)
    A He got fired from his job. He got angry, and Esperanza calmed him down.
    B He won the lottery. He got very excited, and Esperanza translated for him.
    C His mother had died. He begins to cry, and Esperanza holds him.
    D The city was going to demolish the house. Esperanza helped find a new one.

____8. True or False: Aunt Lupe died the day the girls made fun of her.
    A True
    B False

Mango Street Multiple Choice Quiz Questions Page 5

<u>Elenita, Cards, Palm, Water - No Speak English</u>

____1. How does Esperanza describe Elenita? (Elenita, Cards ...)
        A She is like a fairy godmother.
        B She is a gypsy.
        C She is a witch woman.
        D She is an angel.

____2. Esperanza asked about a house. What was Elenita's response? (Elenita, Cards ...)
        A She said, "There's no place like home."
        B She said "Ah, yes, a home in the heart. I see a home in the heart."
        C She said," You will never feel at home anywhere."
        D She said, "Your family is your home."

____3. What happened to Geraldo?
        A He was in a hit and run accident and died.
        B He was deported to Mexico.
        C He was arrested for carrying drugs.
        D He was robbed and beaten by a gang.

____4. What is different about Ruthie? (Edna's Ruthie)
        A She cannot speak.
        B She never leaves the house.
        C She speaks five languages.
        D She is the only adult who likes to play.

____5. What does Esperanza think about Ruthie? (Edna's Ruthie)
        A She thinks Ruthie could have been a lot of things if she had wanted to.
        B She thinks Ruthie is the nicest person she knows.
        C She thinks Ruthie should move out on her own.
        D She thinks Ruthie would be a good mother.

____6. What do all of the children in the neighborhood disagree on regarding Earl? (The Earl of Tennessee)
        A They don't agree about his age.
        B They don't agree about his real name.
        C They don't agree about what his wife looks like.
        D They don't agree on how much money they think he makes.

____7. True or False: Sire and Lois are two mean dogs that scare the children.
        A True
        B False

Mango Street Multiple Choice Quiz Questions Page 6

____8. Who or what are the only ones that understand Esperanza? (Four Skinny Trees)
        A the dogs
        B the flowers
        C the clouds
        D the trees

____9. What broke Mamacita's heart? (No Speak English)
        A Her husband left her for a thin girl.
        B Her husband would not take her out of the house.
        C Her baby boy started singing the Pepsi commercial in English.
        D She found out she could not have any more children.

Mango Street Multiple Choice Quiz Questions Page 7

<u>Rafaela Who Drinks Coconut . . . - What Sally Said</u>

____1. Why does Rafaela's husband lock her in the apartment? (Rafaela...)
      A He thinks she will run away because she is so beautiful.
      B He does not want her to go out and spend money.
      C He is afraid she will go out and get drunk.
      D He does not want her to get a job.

____2. What does Rafaela like to drink? (Rafaela ...)
      A She likes to drink white wine.
      B She likes to drink Coke.
      C She likes to drink coconut and papaya juices.
      D She likes to drink coffee with a lot of sugar.

____3. According to Esperanza, what does Sally want? (Sally)
      A She wants to get married.
      B She wants to love and love and love.
      C She wants to get away from her parents.
      D She wants a boyfriend to make her happy.

____4. True or False: Minerva writes poetry during the day instead of taking care of her children.
      A True
      B False

____5. Why doesn't Esperanza go out with her family on Sundays anymore? (Bums in the Attic)
      A She has too much homework.
      B She does not like the way her father drives.
      C She is busy going out with her friends.
      D She is ashamed of the way they stare out the window at things they can't have.

____6. What does Esperanza say she will do when she is older? (Bums in the Attic)
      A She will own a house and invite the bums in to live in the attic.
      B She will run an orphanage.
      C She will give money to the poor.
      D She will move from city to city and never stay in one place.

____7. What does Esperanza decide about growing up? (Beautiful & Cruel)
      A She wants to be just like her mother.
      B She says she will not grow up tame.
      C She wants to get married right after high school.
      D She will not let anyone stand in the way of her plans.

Mango Street Multiple Choice Quiz Questions Page 8

____8. Who says she used to be smart. She quit school because she did not have nice clothes (Smart ...)
        A Sarita
        B Magdalena
        C Guadalupe
        D Eperanza's mother

____9. True or False: Sally's father caught her talking to a boy and beat her (What Sally Said)
        A True
        B False

Mango Street Multiple Choice Quiz Questions Page 9

<u>The Monkey Garden - Mango Says Good-bye Sometimes</u>

____1. How did Esperanza feel when Sally went into the garden with the boys? (Monkey Garden)
    A She felt depressed.
    B She felt angry.
    C She felt happy.
    D She felt puzzled.

____2. True or False: Esperanza thinks Sally got married to escape. (Linoleum Roses)
    A True
    B False

____3. What does Sally do all day? (Linoleum Roses)
    A She sits and looks out the window and at her possessions.
    B She talks to her friends on the telephone.
    C She reads and writes stories.
    D She eats candy and watches soap operas.

____4. What do the three sisters tell Esperanza? (The Three Sisters)
    A They tell her she will become famous.
    B They tell her she should never get married.
    C They tell her to remember to come back.
    D They tell her she can overcome the past.

____5. True or False: Esperanza is proud of coming from Mango Street. (Alicia & I)
    A True
    B False

____6. Which is **not** in the description of the house Esperanza wants? (A House of My Own)
    A It is a house of her own.
    B It would be quiet and clean.
    C It has a porch and purple petunias.
    D It would be in an upper class neighborhood.

____7. What does Esperanza say she likes to do? (Mango Says Goodbye ...)
    A She likes to paint pictures.
    B She likes to write songs.
    C She likes to tell stories.
    D She likes to watch television.

ANSWER KEY-MULTIPLE CHOICE/QUIZ QUESTIONS

<u>The House on Mango Street - Laughter</u>
1. B
2. C
3. A
4. B FALSE
5. C
6. D
7. A

<u>Gil's Furniture - There Was an Old Woman</u>
1. C
2. A
3. B
4. D
5. C
6. A
7. B

<u>Alicia - Rice Sandwich</u>
1. D
2. A
3. C
4. B
5. C

<u>Chanclas - Born Bad</u>
1. C
2. A
3. B
4. D
5. C
6. A
7. C
8. A

<u>Elenita - No Speak</u>
1. C
2. B
3. A
4. D
5. A
6. C
7. B FALSE
8. D
9. C

<u>Rafaela - What Sally Said</u>
1. A
2. C
3. B
4. B FALSE
5. D
6. A
7. B
8. D
9. A TRUE

<u>Monkey Garden - Mango Says Goodbye</u>
1. B
2. A TRUE
3. A
4. C
5. B FALSE
6. D
7. C

PREREADING VOCABULARY WORKSHEETS

VOCABULARY WORKSHEETS - *House on Mango Street*

The House on Mango Street - Laughter

Part I: Using Prior Knowledge and Context Clues
Below are the sentences in which the vocabulary words appear in the text. Read the sentence. Use any clues you can find in the sentence combined with your prior knowledge, and write what you think the underlined words mean on the lines provided.

1. For the time being, Mama says. ***Temporary***, says Papa.

_____

2. And since she comes right after me, she is my ***responsibility***.

_____

3. Until then I am a red balloon, a balloon tied to an ***anchor***.

_____

4. Just like that, as if she were a fancy ***chandelier***. That's the way he did it.

_____

5. I have inherited her name, but I don't want to ***inherit*** her place by the window.

_____

6. I would like to ***baptize*** myself under a new name, a name more like the real me, the one nobody sees.

_____

7. Cathy's father will have to fly to France one day and find her great great ***distant*** grand cousin on her father's side and inherit the family house.

_____

8. I don't tell them about Nenny just yet. It's too ***complicated***.

_____

Part II: Determining the Meaning   Match the vocabulary words to their dictionary definitions.

___1. temporary   A. duty
___2. responsibility   B. to receive from one who has gone before
___3. anchor   C. to give a first or Christian name to
___4. chandelier   D. heavy object used to keep a boat in place
___5. inherit   E. not easy to understand
___6. baptize   F. for a limited time
___7. distant   G. far apart in relationship
___8. complicated   H. a light fixture that hangs from a ceiling

Mango Street Vocabulary Worksheets Page 2

Gil's Furniture Bought & Sold - There Was an Old Woman . . .
Part I: Using Prior Knowledge and Context Clues
Below are the sentences in which the vocabulary words appear in the text. Read the sentence. Use any clues you can find in the sentence combined with your prior knowledge, and write what you think the underlined words mean on the lines provided.

1. Everything is on top of everything so the whole store has skinny *aisles* to walk through.

_____

2. Or like *marimbas* only with a funny little plucked sound to it like if you were running your fingers across the teeth of a metal comb.

_____

3. Or like marimbas only with a funny little *plucked* sound to it like if you were running your fingers across the teeth of a metal comb.

_____

4. It is wooden. Inside the floors *slant*. Some rooms uphill. Some down.

_____

5. This is the tree we chose for the First *Annual* Tarzan Jumping Contest.

_____

6. The windows didn't roll up like in ordinary cars. Instead there was a button that did it for you *automatically*.

_____

7. She is the one who told us . . . if you count the white *flecks* on your fingernails you can know how many boys are thinking of you and lots of other things I can't remember now.

_____

8. . . . and didn't even stop Refugia from getting her head stuck between two *slats* in the back gate and nobody looked up . . .

_____

Mango Street Vocabulary Worksheets Page 3

<u>Gil's Furniture Bought & Sold - There Was an Old Woman . . .</u>
Part II: Determining the Meaning   Match the vocabulary words to their dictionary definitions.

____1. aisles   A. done every year
____2. marimbas   B. sloped; made diagonal
____3. plucked   C. a wooden, xylophone-like instrument
____4. slant   D. tiny spots
____5. annual   E. done by machine
____6. automatically   F. passageways in a store or theater
____7. flecks   G. narrow strips of wood or metal
____8. slats   H. removed with the fingers

ango Street Vocabulary Worksheets Page 4

Alicia Who Sees Mice - A Rice Sandwich
Part I: Using Prior Knowledge and Context Clues
Below are the sentences in which the vocabulary words appear in the text. Read the sentence. Use any clues you can find in the sentence combined with your prior knowledge, and write what you think the underlined words mean on the lines provided.

1. That up there, that's ***cumulus***, and everybody looks up.

_____

2. And don't forget ***nimbus*** the rain cloud, I add, that's something.

_____

3. The mother's feet, plump and polite, ***descended*** like white pigeons from the sea of the pillow, across the linoleum roses, down the wooden stairs, over the chalk hopscotch squares .

_____

4. The mother's feet, plump and polite, descended like white pigeons from the sea of the pillow, across the ***linoleum*** roses, down the wooden stairs, over the chalk hopscotch squares . . . .

_____

5. It's Rachel who learned to walk the best all ***strutted*** in those magic high heels.

_____

6. The special kids, the ones who wear keys around their necks, get to eat in the ***canteen***.

_____

7. I'm no Spartan and hold up an ***anemic*** wrist to prove it.

_____

Part II: Determining the Meaning Match the vocabulary words to their dictionary definitions.

____1. cumulus   A. weak; without much energy
____2. nimbus   B. a washable floor covering
____3. descended   C. a low, dark rain cloud
____4. linoleum   D. walked in a pompous way; swaggered
____5. strutted   E. went down
____6. canteen   F. white, fluffy clouds with a flat base
____7. anemic   G. a small cafeteria or snack bar

Mango Street Vocabulary Worksheets Page 5

Chanclas - Born Bad
Part I: Using Prior Knowledge and Context Clues
Below are the sentences in which the vocabulary words appear in the text. Read the sentence. Use any clues you can find in the sentence combined with your prior knowledge, and write what you think the underlined words mean on the lines provided.

1. My feet swell big and heavy like *plungers*, but I drag them across the linoleum floor . . . .
_____

2. Ready and waiting like a new Buick with the keys in the *ignition*. Ready to take you where?
_____

3. She is the color of a bar of *naphtha* laundry soap, she is like the little brown piece left at the end of the wash, the hard little bone, my sister.
_____

4. I came home . . . all wet because Tito had pushed me into the open water *hydrant* . . . .
_____

5. Like sticky *capsules* filled with jelly
_____

Part II: Determining the Meaning   Match the vocabulary words to their dictionary definitions.

____1. plungers   A. the switch that turns on a car
____2. ignition   B. an upright cylinder for holding water
____3. naphtha   C. a kind of soap
____4. hydrant   D. a small, oval shaped, jelly-like container
____5. capsules   E. rubber suction cups on sticks

Not tested:
Or *merengue*. a rapid dance
Or *tembleque*! a dance; a hair ornament
Your *abuelito* is dead, Papa says early one morning in my room. *Está muerto* . . . .

Mango Street Vocabulary Worksheets Page 6

<u>Elenita, Cards, Palm, Water - No Speak English</u>
Part I: Using Prior Knowledge and Context Clues
Below are the sentences in which the vocabulary words appear in the text. Read the sentence. Use any clues you can find in the sentence combined with your prior knowledge, and write what you think the underlined words mean on the lines provided.

1. Golden *goblets*, sad-looking women dressed in old-fashioned dresses, and roses that cry.

_____

2. Here a *pillar* of bees and this a mattress of luxury.

_____

3. Here a pillar of bees and this a mattress of *luxury*.

_____

4. Nobody but an *intern* working all alone.

_____

5. And maybe if the *surgeon* would've come, maybe if he hadn't lost so much blood, if the surgeon had only come, they would know who to notify and where.

_____

6. They never knew about the two-room *flats* and sleeping rooms he rented . . .

_____

7. . . . the weekly money orders sent home, the *currency* exchanged.

_____

8. Their strength is their secret. They send *ferocious* roots beneath the ground.

_____

9. ¡Ay! Mamacita, who does not belong, every once in a while lets out a cry, *hysterical*, high, as if he had torn the only skinny thread that kept her alive, the only road out to that country.

_____

Mango Street Vocabulary Worksheets Page 7

Elenita, Cards, Palm, Water - No Speak English
Part II: Determining the Meaning   Match the vocabulary words to their dictionary definitions.

____1. goblets	A. a column or vertical support
____2. pillar	B. uncontrolled laughing or crying
____3. luxury	C. an advanced student
____4. intern	D. money
____5. surgeon	E. savage, fierce
____6. flats	F. a doctor who operates on patients
____7. currency	G. a type of glass with a stem and a base
____8. ferocious	H. an apartment all on one floor
____9. hysterical	I. comfort and pleasure

Good, she says, los *espíritus* are here. *The spirits.*
¿*Cuándo, cuándo, cuándo*? she asks. *When, when, when?*

Mango Street Vocabulary Worksheets Page 8

Rafaela Who Drinks Coconut . . . - What Sally Said
Part I: Using Prior Knowledge and Context Clues
Below are the sentences in which the vocabulary words appear in the text. Read the sentence. Use any clues you can find in the sentence combined with your prior knowledge, and write what you think the underlined words mean on the lines provided.

1. The boys at school think she's beautiful because her hair is shiny black like *raven* feathers ....

_____

2. They don't look down at all except to be content to live on hills.

_____

3. I'll offer them the *attic*, then ask them to stay, because I know how it is to be without a house.

_____

4. . . . But I have decided not to grow up tame like the others who lay their necks on the *threshold* waiting for the ball and chain.

_____

Part II: Determining the Meaning   Match the vocabulary words to their dictionary definitions.

    ____1. raven   A. a room directly below the roof
    ____2. content   B. satisfied
    ____3. attic   C. an entrance or doorway
    ____4. threshold   D. a large bird with black feathers

Look at my *comadres*. She means Izaura whose husband left and Yolanda whose husband is dead.

Mango Street Vocabulary Worksheets Page 9

<u>The Monkey Garden - Mango Says Goodbye Sometimes</u>
Part I: Using Prior Knowledge and Context Clues
Below are the sentences in which the vocabulary words appear in the text. Read the sentence. Use any clues you can find in the sentence combined with your prior knowledge, and write what you think the underlined words mean on the lines provided.

1. The monkey doesn't live there anymore... And I was glad because I couldn't listen anymore to his wild screaming at night, the ***twangy*** yakkety-yak of the people who owned him.

_____

2. She met a marshmallow salesman at a school ***bazaar***, and married him in another state . . . .

_____

3. I say, "and so she ***trudged*** up the wooden stairs, her sad brown shoes taking her to the house she never liked."

_____

Part II: Determining the Meaning   Match the vocabulary words to their dictionary definitions.

____1. twangy   A. walked in a heavy-footed way; plodded
____2. bazaar   B. a fair or sale
____3. trudged   C. a sharp, vibrating sound

ANSWER KEY: VOCABULARY WORKSHEETS - *House on Mango Street*

House on Mango Street-Laughter
1. F
2. A
3. D
4. H
5. B
6. C
7. G
8. E

Chanclas-Born Bad
1. E
2. A
3. C
4. B
5. D

Gil's Furniture-There Was An Old Woman
1. F
2. C
3. H
4. B
5. A
6. E
7. D
8. G

Elenita-No Speak English
1. G
2. A
3. I
4. C
5. F
6. H
7. D
8. E
9. B

Alicia Who Sees Mice-A Rice Sandwich
1. F
2. C
3. E
4. B
5. D
6. G
7. A

Rafaela-What Sally Said
1. D
2. B
3. A
4. C

Monkey-Mango
1. C
2. B
3. A

DAILY LESSON PLANS

LESSON ONE

Student Objectives
1. To receive books and other related materials (study guides, reading assignment)
2. To relate prior knowledge to the new material
3. To develop research skills
4. To write to inform by developing and organizing facts to convey information
5. To begin Writing Assignment #1 and the Nonfiction assignment

Activity #1

Show students pictures of barrio life in a major city such as Los Angeles or Chicago. Then do a group KWL Sheet with the students. Some students will know something about Sandra Cisneros or *The House on Mango Street* and will have information to share. Put this information in the K column (What I Know.) Ask students what they want to find out from reading the book and record this in the W column (What I Want to Find Out.) Keep the sheet and refer back to it after reading the book. Complete the L column (What I Learned) at that time.

Activity #2

Distribute the materials students will use in this unit. Explain in detail how students are to use these materials.

Study Guides Students should preview the study guide questions before each reading assignment to get a feeling for what events and ideas are important in that section. After reading the section, students will (as a class or individually) answer the questions to review the important events and ideas from that section of the book. Students should keep the study guides as study materials for the unit test.

Reading / Writing Assignment Sheet You need to fill in the reading and writing assignment sheet to let students know when their reading has to be completed. You can either write the assignment sheet on a side blackboard or bulletin board and leave it there for students to see each day, or you can duplicate copies for each student to have. In either case, you should advise students to become very familiar with the reading assignments so they know what is expected of them.

Unit Outline You may find it helpful to distribute copies of the Unit Outline to your students so they can keep track of upcoming lessons and assignments. You may also want to post a copy of the Unit Outline on a bulletin board and cross off each lesson as you complete it.

Extra Activities Center The Unit Resource portion of this unit contains suggestions for a library of related books and articles in your classroom as well as crossword and word search puzzles. Make an extra activities center in your room where you will keep these materials for students to use. Bring the books and articles in from the library and keep several copies of the puzzles on hand. Explain to students that these materials are available for students to use when they finish reading assignments or other class work early.

Books Each school has its own rules and regulations regarding student use of school books. Advise students of the procedures that are normal for your school.

Notebook or Unit Folder You may want the students to keep all of their worksheets, notes, and other papers for the unit together in a binder or notebook. During the first class meeting, tell them how you want them to arrange the folder. Make divider pages for vocabulary worksheets, prereading study guide questions, review activities, notes, and tests. You may want to give a grade for accuracy in keeping the folder.

Activity #3

Assign one of the following topics (or topics of your choice) to each of the students. Distribute Writing Assignment #1 and the Nonfiction Assignment sheet and discuss them. Students should fill this out the Nonfiction Assignment sheet for at least one of the sources they used and submit it along with their report.

Suggested Topics
1. The traditional and changing roles of women in Latino culture.
2. The traditional and changing roles of men in Latino culture.
3. The history of Hispanic inhabitants and culture in the United States.
4. Barrio life in Chicago, Los Angeles, or any other major city.
5. Multiculturalism in the United States.
6. Chicano / Chicana writers.
7. Immigration from Mexico to the United States.
8. Hispanic America mourning and burial ceremonies and practices.

KWL

Directions: Before reading, think about what you already know about Sandra Cisneros and/or *The House on Mango Street*. Write the information in the **K** column. Think about what you would like to find out from reading the book. Write your questions in the **W** column. After you have read the book, use the **L** column to write the answers to your questions from the W column, and anything else you remember from the book.

K	**W**	**L**
What I Know	**What I Want to Find Out**	**What I Learned**

WRITING ASSIGNMENT #1 - *House on Mango Street*

PROMPT

You are reading a semi-autobiographical novel about the life of a young Hispanic American girl. The setting is present day, in the Latino section of Chicago. In order to better understand the novel, you must first understand more about the author / narrator's cultural heritage and background.

PREWRITING

Your teacher may assign a topic or allow you to choose one. You will then go to the library to research the topic. Look for encyclopedias, books, magazine articles, videos, and Internet sources. You may want to interview an expert on the topic of your choice.

Think of questions you have about your topic. Write each one on a separate index card. Then read to find the answers, and write them on the cards. Also take notes on interesting and important facts, even if you did not have questions about them. Put each fact on a separate card. Make sure to cite your references. That means to write down the title of the book or article, the author, and the page number for each one.

Arrange your note card in the order you want to use for your paper. Number them, perhaps in the upper right hand corner. Read through them to make sure they make sense in that order. Rearrange as necessary.

DRAFTING

Introduce your topic in the first paragraph. Tell why you chose it, and give a preview of what the rest of the paper will be about. Then write several paragraphs about the topic. Each paragraph should have a main idea and supporting details. Your last paragraph should summarize the information in the report.

PEER CONFERENCE/REVISING

When you finish the rough draft, ask another student to look at it. You may want to give the student your note cards so he/she can double check for you and see that you have included all of the information. After reading, he or she should tell you what he/she liked best about your report, which parts were difficult to understand or needed more information, and ways in which your work could be improved. Reread your report considering your critic's comments and make the corrections you think are necessary.

PROOFREADING/EDITING

Do a final proofreading of your report, double-checking your grammar, spelling, organization, and the clarity of your ideas.

PUBLISHING

Follow your teacher's directions for making a final copy of your report.

WRITING EVALUATION - *The House on Mango Street*

Name _____ Date _____ Class _____

Writing Assignment # _____

Circle One For Each Item:

<u>Composition</u>	excellent	good	fair	poor
<u>Style</u>	excellent	good	fair	poor
<u>Grammar</u>	excellent	good	fair	poor
<u>Spelling</u>	excellent	good	fair	poor
<u>Punctuation</u>	excellent	good	fair	poor
<u>Legibility</u>	excellent	good	fair	poor

<u>Strengths:</u>

<u>Weaknesses:</u>

<u>Comments/Suggestions:</u>

NONFICTION ASSIGNMENT SHEET - *House on Mango Street*
(To be completed after reading the required nonfiction article)

Name _____ Date _____ Class/ _____

Title of Nonfiction Read _____

Author _____ Publication Date _____

I. **Factual Summary:** Write a short summary of the piece you read.

II. **Vocabulary:**
   1. Which vocabulary words were difficult?

   2. What did you do to help yourself understand the words?

III. **Interpretation:** What was the main point the author wanted you to get from reading his/her work?

IV. **Criticism:**
   1. Which points of the piece did you agree with or find easy to believe? Why?

   2. With which points of the piece did you disagree or find difficult to believe? Why?

V. **Personal Response:**
   1. What do you think about this piece?

   2. How does this piece help you better understand the novel *The House on Mango Street?*

LESSON TWO

Objectives
1. To discuss the form and genre of the novel
2. To become familiar with the vocabulary for chapters titled "The House on Mango Street" through "Laughter"
3. To preview the study questions for chapters titled "The House on Mango Street" through "Laughter"
4. To read chapters titled "The House on Mango Street" through "Laughter"

Activity #1
Tell students that critics of the novel as well as literature scholars disagree on the genre of the book. Make sure students understand the characteristics of the following genres: children's literature, short story, novel, essay, autobiography, poetry, women's studies, ethnic literature. Tell students to think of these as they read, and form a conclusion as to where they would place the book.

Activity #2
Work through the prereading vocabulary worksheet with the students. Tell them they will have a sheet like this to complete before reading each section of the book.

Activity #3
Show students how to preview the study questions. Encourage students to predict what they think answers might be, to write down their predictions, and to compare these with their answers after reading the chapters.

Activity #4
You may want to read "The House on Mango Street" aloud to the students to set the mood for the novel. Invite willing students to read successive chapters aloud to the rest of the class.

LESSON THREE

Objectives
1. To discuss the main ideas an events in chapters titled "The House on Mango Street" through "Laughter"
2. To understand the concept of voice in the novel

Activity #1

Discuss the answers to the Study Guide questions for chapters titled "The House on Mango Street" through "Laughter" in detail. Write the answers on the board or overhead projector so students can have the correct answers for study purposes. Encourage students to take notes. If the students own their books, encourage them to use high lighter pens to mark important passages and the answers to the study guide questions.

Note: It is a good practice in public speaking and leadership skills for individual students to take charge of leading the discussion of the study questions. Perhaps a different student could go to the front of the class and lead the discussion each day that the study questions are discussed during this unit. Of course, the teacher should guide the discussion when appropriate and be sure to fill in any gaps the students leave.

Activity #2 Minilesson: Voice

Tell students that voice it the quality of a piece of writing that makes it the author's own. Writers work to develop a distinct, individual voice. When Sandra Cisneros was enrolled in the Iowa Writer's Workshop in the late 1970s, she was the only Mexican American woman in the group. She realized that she could not write in the same way as her classmates, because her life experiences as a poor girl living in a barrio were so different from what they had experienced. She began to write about the things she knew, and developed her own voice. Ask students to listen for the voice in the novel as they read.

LESSON FOUR

Objectives
1. To become familiar with the vocabulary for chapters titled "Gil's Furniture Bought and Sold" through "There Was an Old Woman . . ."
2. To preview the study questions
3. To read the chapters

Activity #1

Have students work in small groups to complete the prereading vocabulary worksheet. They can also discuss the study guide questions, and predict answers.

Activity #2

Have students read the chapters aloud or silently, depending on their needs and abilities. You may want to let the quicker students read ahead silently while you conduct an oral reading of the story with the students who need more guidance.

LESSON FIVE

Objectives
1. To discuss the main ideas and events in chapters titled "Gil's Furniture Bought and Sold" through "There Was an Old Woman . . ."
2. To understand character development by discussing Esperanza's character

Activity #1
Invite volunteers to briefly summarize each chapter. Then have them give the answers to the study guide questions. Encourage students to look back through the chapters to find any answers they missed.

Activity #2 Minilesson: Character
Explain that an author creates a character, in this case Esperanza Cordero, by giving her traits such as physical attributes, thoughts, and feelings. The author develops these traits by telling what the character says, does, and thinks. Writers usually base their characters at least in part on a real person or persons, and then elaborate. (The life of the narrator, Esperanza Cordero, is in many ways similar to that of Sandra Cisneros.) A good writer will make the characters believable for the readers.

Explain that this is a "coming-of-age" story, where the central character becomes more aware of herself because of events that occur. In this novel, the awareness comes because of Esperanza's experiences growing up in the barrio neighborhood in Chicago.

Have students look for Esperanza's character traits as they begin reading. After they have read the first three chapters, help them begin filling in the Character Trait Chart. Tell them they should continue to be aware of Esperanza's character as they read, and that they will continue the discussion and complete more of the chart during Lesson 16.

LESSON SIX

Objectives
    1. To become familiar with the vocabulary for chapters titled "Alicia Who Sees Mice" through "A Rice Sandwich"
    2. To preview the study questions
    3. To read the chapters
    4. To read aloud for evaluation

Activity #1

    Give students ten or fifteen minutes to complete the prereading vocabulary worksheet and preview the study guide questions.

Activity #2

    Tell students their oral reading ability will be evaluated. Show them copies of the Oral Reading Evaluation Form and discuss it. Model correct intonation and expression by reading the first few paragraphs of "Alicia Who Sees Mice" aloud.

Activity #3

    Call on individual students to read a few paragraphs aloud. Encourage the other students to follow along silently in their books. If you have a student who is unwilling or unable to read in front of the group make arrangements to do his or her evaluation privately at another time.

CHARACTER TRAITS CHART - *House on Mango Street*

Character Trait _____
Events That Show It:

Character Trait _____
Events That Show It:

Character Trait _____
Events That Show It:

Character Trait _____
Events That Show It:

ORAL READING EVALUATION - *House on Mango Street*

Name_____   Class_____ Date _____

SKILL	EXCELLENT	GOOD	AVERAGE	FAIR	POOR
FLUENCY	5	4	3	2	1
CLARITY	5	4	3	2	1
AUDIBILITY	5	4	3	2	1
PRONUNCIATION	5	4	3	2	1
_____	5	4	3	2	1
_____	5	4	3	2	1

TOTAL _____   **GRADE** _____

COMMENTS:

LESSON SEVEN

Objectives
1. To discuss the main ideas and events from "Alicia Who Sees Mice" to "A Rice Sandwich"
2. To become familiar with the vocabulary for chapters titled "Chanclas" through "Born Bad"
3. To preview the study questions
4. To read the chapters

Activity #1

Give each student four 1"x2" strips of colored paper or index cards--one blue, one yellow, one green, one pink. Have them put a large letter A on the blue paper, B on the yellow, C on the green, and D on the pink. Distribute copies of the Multiple Choice/Quiz questions for the chapters. Ask students to read the first question and hold up the colored paper for the correct answer. Then have them mark the correct answer on their worksheets.

Activity #2

Write the five vocabulary words on the board. Ask students if they already know the meanings of any of the words. Invite students to guess the meanings, and list them on the board. Then have them complete the prereading vocabulary worksheet. Compare students' guesses with the actual meanings. Ask volunteers to use the words in sentences.

Activity #3

Give students the rest of the class time to read the chapters silently and answer the study questions.

LESSON EIGHT

Objectives
    1. To discuss the main ideas and events in chapters titled "Chanclas" through "Born Bad"
    2. To identify types of figurative language in the novel

Activity #1

    Have small groups of students choose one of the questions and prepare a two-minute skit to answer the question. After all groups have presented their skits, go over students' written answers to the questions.

Activity #2 Minilesson: Figures of Speech

    Figures of speech are literary devices that give the writer a non-literal way to describe images and events. Use the following chart to give examples of the different figures of speech. Then write "My papa's hair is like a broom, all up in the air" on the board. (Esperanza uses this description of her father's hair on page 6, "Hairs" of *The House on Mango Street*. Ask students to identify the type of figure of speech (simile.) Talk about the literal meaning. Distribute the Figure of Speech worksheet and have students work in small groups to find examples in the novel. If you want the students to continue recording examples in the remaining chapters, assign a due date for the worksheet.

    Example from the novel:
Until then I am a red balloon, a balloon tied to an anchor. "Boys & Girls"

FIGURES OF SPEECH

<u>CLICHÉ</u>	A cliché is an expression that has been used repeatedly, and has lost its appeal. For example: *white as snow, bright and early.*
<u>HYPERBOLE</u>	Extreme exaggeration used to describe a person or thing. For example: *She had as many pairs of shoes as there are stars in the sky.*
<u>IRONY</u>	The use of words to express something different from and often opposite to their literal meaning.
<u>METAPHOR</u>	A comparison without the words like or as. For example, *The cat is a bag of bones.*
<u>METONYMY</u>	A figure of speech in which one word or phrase is substituted for another with which it is closely associated, as in the use of *Washington* for the United States government or of *the sword* for military power.
<u>ONOMATOPOEIA</u>	The use of words such as *buzz* or *splash* that imitate the sounds associated with the objects or actions they refer to.
<u>PARADOX</u>	A seemingly self-contradictory statement that has some truth to it.
<u>PERSONIFICATION</u>	Attributing human characteristics to inanimate objects, animals, or ideas, as in *the wind howled.*
<u>SIMILE</u>	A comparison using the words like or as.

FIGURES OF SPEECH

Figures of speech are literary devices that give the writer a non-literal way to describe images and events. The main types of figures of speech are hyperbole, irony, metaphor, metonymy, onomatopoeia, paradox, personification, and simile. Use the following chart to record examples of figures of speech used in *The House on Mango Street*. A sample has been done for you. Note: You may not find an example of each figure of speech in the novel.

Figure of Speech   **Example from Novel, page #**   **Literal Meaning**

LESSON NINE

Objective
To write a persuasive argument

Activity #1
Ask students if they have ever had someone try to persuade them to do something, such as a parent persuading them to eat an unfamiliar food or do a chore they don't want to do. Invite a few pairs of students to role-play such situations. Tell students they will be writing a persuasive argument based on the novel.

Activity #2
Distribute copies of Writing Assignment #2. Go over it in detail with students. Give them the rest of the class period to complete the assignment. You may want to have students present their papers orally.

Activity #3
Tell students they will have a quiz during the next class period on the chapters they have read so far.

LESSON TEN

Objectives
1. To take a quiz on the chapters read so far
2. To become familiar with the vocabulary for chapters titled "Elenita . . . " through "No Speak English"
3. To preview the study questions
4. To read the chapters

Activity #1
Distribute copies of the multiple choice study/quiz questions. Give students about fifteen minutes to answer the questions. Collect the papers.

Activity #2
Give students about fifteen minutes to complete the prereading vocabulary worksheet and go over the study guide questions.

Activity #3
Play a "Password" type game using the vocabulary words. Divide students into teams and have each team choose a player to start. Player A gives clues for a word to the Player B. If Player B guesses the word, team B gets a point. Play continues until all of the words have been used.

Give students the rest of the class period to read the assigned chapters.

WRITING ASSIGNMENT #2 - *House on Mango Street*

PROMPT

There are many occasions in the novel when one character tries to persuade another to do or not do something. For example, Uncle Nacho tries to persuade Esperanza to dance, and Esperanza persuades her mother to let her stay at school for lunch. Your assignment is to choose one situation from the novel, take the part of one of the characters, and persuade another character to do or not do something.

PREWRITING

First, choose the characters and the situation. Write down what you want or don't want the other person to do. Then make a list of your reasons or arguments. Think of statements to support each of your reasons, and list them under each reason. Then number the reasons in order from most to least important.

DRAFTING

Make an introductory statement in which you state your desire. Use one paragraph for each of your reasons. Use the supporting statements for each reason. Summarize your request.

PEER CONFERENCING/REVISING

When you finish the rough draft, ask another student to look at it. You may want to give the student your checklist so he/she can double check for you and see that you have included all of the information. After reading, he or she should tell you what he/she liked best about your persuasive letter, which parts were difficult to understand or needed more information, and ways in which your work could be improved. Reread your persuasive letter considering your critic's comments and make the corrections you think are necessary.

PROOFREADING/EDITING

Do a final proofreading of your persuasive letter, double-checking your grammar, spelling, organization, and the clarity of your ideas.

FINAL DRAFT

Follow your teacher's guidelines for completing the final draft of your paper.

PUBLISHING

Follow your teacher's guidelines for publishing your work.

LESSON ELEVEN

Objectives
    1. To participate in a writing conference with the teacher
    2. To become familiar with the vocabulary for chapters titled "Rafaela . . ." through "What Sally Said"
    3. To preview the study questions
    4. To read the chapters

Activity #1

    Assign the vocabulary and reading work. Ask students to work independently while you hold the writing conferences. Tell them that the answers to study guide questions for chapters from "Elenita" through "What Sally Said" will be due at the beginning of the next class period.

Activity #2

    Hold individual writing conferences in a quiet corner of the room.

LESSON TWELVE

Objectives
    1. To discuss the main ideas and details in chapters from "Elenita" through "No Speak English" and Rafaela . . ." through "What Sally Said"
    2. To become familiar with the vocabulary for chapters titled "The Monkey Garden" through "Mango Says Goodbye Sometimes"
    3. To preview the study questions
    4. To read the chapters

Activity #1

    Divide students into small groups and have them go over the answers to the study questions. Circulate among groups and answer any questions they have.

Activity #2

    While students are still in the groups, have them complete the prereading vocabulary worksheet and go over the study guide questions for the chapters titled "The Monkey Garden" through "Mango Says Goodbye Sometimes."

Activity #3

    Ask for volunteers to read the chapters aloud. Tell the rest of the students to follow along in their books.

LESSON THIRTEEN

Objectives
1. To discuss the main ideas and events in chapters titled "The Monkey Garden" through "Mango Says Goodbye Sometimes"
2. To discuss *The House on Mango Street* at the interpretive and critical levels

Activity #1
Briefly go over the answers to the study guide questions. Ask volunteers to contribute the answers.

Activity #2
Choose the questions from the Extra Writing Assignments/Discussion Questions which seem most appropriate for your students. A class discussion of these questions is most effective if students have been given the opportunity to formulate answers to the questions prior to the discussion. To this end, you may either have all the students formulate answers to all the questions, divide the class into groups and assign one or more questions to each group, or you could assign one question to each student in your class. The option you choose will make a difference in the amount of class time needed for this activity.

Activity #3
After students have had ample time to formulate answers to the questions, begin your class discussion of the questions and the ideas presented by the questions. Be sure students take notes during the discussion so they have information to study for the unit test.

LESSON FOURTEEN

Objective
To write to express a personal opinion

Activity #1
Ask students if they have ever written in a journal or diary, or otherwise kept a record of their lives. Invite volunteers to share their experiences with the class. Tell students they will be writing an autobiographical sketch similar to one of the chapters in the novel.

Activity #2
Distribute copies of Writing Assignment #3 and go over it in detail with students. Give them the rest of the class period to work on the assignment. If it is not finished in class, assign a due date.

EXTRA DISCUSSION QUESTIONS - *House on Mango Street*

<u>Interpretive</u>

1. How did the narrator feel when the nun saw her house? (The House on Mango Street)

2. How does the narrator feel about the house on Mango Street?

3. The boys don't talk to the girls outside of the house. What does this say about the lifestyle/culture of the narrator? (Boys & Girls)

4. What does the narrator mean when she says she is "a red balloon, a balloon tied to an anchor"?

5. What does Esperanza mean when she says she does not want to inherit her great-grandmother's place by the window? (My Name)

6. Why does Esperanza want to baptize herself under a new name? (My Name)

7. How do you think Esperanza feels when Cathy says the neighborhood is getting bad? (Cathy Queen of Cats)

8. Esperanza chipped in for the bike even though she knew it would make Cathy mad. What does this reveal about her character? (Our Good Day)

9. Explain the way Esperanza says she and Nenny look like sisters. (Laughter)

10. Why did the incident with the music box make Esperanza feel stupid? (Gil's Furniture)

11. Why do you think the old man would not sell the music box? (Gil's Furniture)

12. How do you think Esperanza feels about Marin? (Marin)

13. What social comment is Esperanza making in "Those Who Don't"?

14. Why don't the neighbors care about the Vargas children? (There Was an Old Woman)

15. Why does Alicia's father say there aren't any mice? (Alicia Who Sees Mice)

16. Why didn't the girls complain when Lucy's mother threw out the shoes? (The Family of Little Feet)

17. What do you think Esperanza expected when she ate in the canteen? What happened? (a Rice Sandwich)

18. Does Uncle Nacho realize how Esperanza feels about the shoes? (Chanclas)

19. How does Esperanza seem to feel about Nenny? (Hips)

20. What does Esperanza's behavior in "Papa Who Wakes Up ..." tell about her ?

21. How do you think the girls felt when they found out Aunt Lupe had died? (Born Bad)

22. How does Esperanza feel after her visit to the witch woman? (Elenita, Cards ..)

23. What do you think "a home in the heart" means? (Elenita, Cards, ...)

24. What else is Esperanza telling us about Geraldo? (Geraldo)

25. Why do you think Ruthie lives the way she does? (Edna's Ruthie)

26. Why did Sandra Cisneros call the chapter "Edna's Ruthie" instead of "Ruthie"?

27. What does Esperanza's comparison of herself to the trees say about her? (Four Skinny Trees)

28. Why doesn't Mamacita want to speak English? (No Speak English)

29. What is the symbolism of the sweet drinks that Rafaela drinks? (Rafaela ...)

30. What does the phrase "Eyes like Egypt" mean? (Sally)

31. What kind of life does Sally have? (Sally)

32. Discuss the symbolism of the threshold. (Beautiful & Cruel)

33. What statement is Esperanza making by leaving the table like a man? ((Beautiful & Cruel)

34. How did the garden change for Esperanza? What does this symbolize? (Monkey Garden)

35. What is the mood in "Red Clowns"?

36. Why is a house so important to Esperanza? (A House of My Own)

Critical

37. With what issues does the book deal? Does it do so in a realistic way?

38. How would you classify the book? To which genre (children's literature, short story, novel, essay, poetry) do you think it belongs? Why?

39. What is Cisneros saying about women in general, and Hispanic women in particular?

40. Is the use of the child's voice effective? Why or why not?

41. What does the book show about gender-class-race relations?

42. How does the narrator begin to change in the chapter titled "Beautiful and Cruel"?

43. The book begins and ends the same way. Is this an effective plot device?

44. From what point of view is the story written? How does this affect our understanding of the story?

45. What are the main conflicts in the story? Are they resolved? If so, how? If not, why not?

46. What is the setting? How important is the setting to the story? Why?

47. Is the story believable? Why or why not?

48. How did Esperanza change over the course of the novel? Were these changes for the better?

49. Was the character of Esperanza believable? Why or why not?

50. Sandra Cisneros often used vivid language to describe a scene or event. Give an example of her use of vivid language that you found most effective. Tell why it was effective.

51. What was the overall mood of the story? Give examples to support your answer.

52. Does the mood of the story change? How does the author show this?

53. What words does the author use to create the atmosphere of the book?

54. Which chapter was most important? Why?

55. Were the descriptions in the book effective? Give some examples.

56. Which senses did the descriptions cause you to use? Give examples of the descriptions using hearing, seeing, touching, smelling, taste.

Personal Opinion

57. Why do you think the author included a chapter describing the hair of all of the family members?

58. What kind of image does the narrator's description in "Hairs" bring to mind?

59. Why do you think Esperanza chose the name "Zeze the X" for herself? (My Name)

60. Esperanza says she won't come back to Mango Street until somebody makes it better. Who can make it better? (Alicia & I ...)

61. Did you enjoy reading *The House on Mango Street?* Why or why not?

62. Is *The House on Mango Street* a good title for the book? Why or why not? If not, what title would you suggest?

63. What do you think Esperanza will do next?

64. If you were Esperanza, what would you do about living on Mango Street?

65. Did you have strong feelings while reading this book? If so, what did the author do to cause those feelings? If not, why not?

66. Will you read more of Sandra Cisneros's books? Why or why not?

67. Did Esperanza's experiences change the way you look at yourself? How?

68. Have you read any other stories similar to *The House on Mango Street?* If so, tell about them.

69. Would you recommend this book to another student? Why or why not?

70. What makes Sandra Cisneros a unique and different author?

71. What questions would you like to ask the author?

72. What was the funniest part of the story? What was the saddest part? What was the most exciting part?

73. What do you remember most about the story?

74. What picture did the author leave in your mind?

75. What did the book make you think about?

76. Sandra Cisneros says the book is semi-autobiographical. What are the advantages and disadvantages of using a narrator who is not the author in a novel of this style? Is it more or less effective than writing an autobiography?

77. Are the chapter titles effective? How well do they relate to the content of the chapters?

QUOTATIONS - *House on Mango Street*

Discuss the significance of the following quotations.

1. "But the house on Mango Street is not the way they told it at all." (The House on Mango ...)

2. "For the time being, mama says. Temporary, says Papa. But I know how those things go." (The House on Mango Street)

3. "Until then I am a red balloon, a balloon tied to an anchor. (Boys & Girls)

4. "I would like to baptize myself under a new name, a name more like the real me, the one nobody sees." (My Name)

5. "In the meantime they'll just have to move a little farther north from Mango Street, a little farther away every time people like us keep moving in." (Cathy Queen of Cats)

6. "Nenny says: Yes, that's Mexico all right. That's what I was thinking exactly." (Laughter)

7. "And then I don't know why, but I have to turn around and pretend I don't care about the box so Nenny won't see how stupid I am." (Gil's Furniture Bought and Sold)

8. "Marin, under the streetlight, dancing by herself, is singing the same song somewhere. I know. Is waiting for a car to stop, a star to fall, someone to change her life." (Marin)

9. "All brown all around, we are safe. But watch us drive into a neighborhood of another color and our knees go shakity-shake and our car windows get rolled up tight and our eyes look straight." (Those Who Don't)

10. "But after a while you get tired of being worried about kids who aren't even yours. (There Was an Old Woman She Had So Many Children She Didn't Know What to Do)

11. "You can never have too much sky." (Darius & the Clouds)

12. "In the canteen, which was nothing special, lots of boys and girls watched while I cried and ate my sandwich, the bread already greasy and the rice cold." (A Rice Sandwich)

13. "My uncle and me bow and he walks me back in my thick shoes to my mother who is proud to be my mother." (Chanclas)

14. "One day you wake up and they are there. Ready and waiting like a new Buick with the keys in the ignition. Ready to take you where?" (Hips)

15. "And I think if my own Papa died what I would do. I hold my Papa in my arms. I hold and hold and hold him." (Papa Who Wakes Up Tired in the Dark)

16. "Most likely I will go to hell and most likely I deserve to be there." (Born Bad)

17. "What about a house, I say, because that's what I came for.
    Ah, yes, a home in the heart. I see a home in the heart.
    Is that *it*?
    That's what I see, she says, then gets up because her kids are fighting." (Elenita ...)

18. "They never saw the kitchenettes. They never knew about the two-room flats and sleeping rooms he rented, the weekly money orders sent home, the currency exchange. How could they? (Geraldo No Last Name)

19. "There were many things Ruthie could have been if she wanted to." (Edna's Ruthie)

20. "When I am too sad and too skinny to keep keeping, when I am a tiny thing against so many bricks, then it is I look at trees. When there is nothing left to look at on this street. Four who grew despite concrete. Four who reach and do not forget to reach. Four whose only reason is to be and be. (Four Skinny Trees)

21. "My father says when he came to this country he ate hamandeggs for three months. Breakfast, lunch, and dinner. Hamandeggs. That was the only word he knew. He doesn't eat hamandeggs anymore." (No Speak English)

22. "And always there is someone offering sweeter drinks, someone promising to keep them on a silver string." (Rafaela....)

23. "Sally, do you sometimes wish you didn't have to go home?" (Sally)

24. "I don't know which way she'll go. There is nothing *I* can do." (Minerva Writes Poems)

25. "Rats? they'll ask.
    Bums, I'll say, and I'll be happy." (Bums in the Attic)

26. "I have begun my own quiet war. Simple. Sure. I am one who leaves the table like a man, without putting back the chair or picking up the plate." (Beautiful & Cruel)

27. "Who was it that said I was getting too old to play the games? Who was it I didn't listen to? I only remember that when the others ran, I wanted to run too, up and down and through the monkey garden, fast as the boys, not like Sally who screamed if she got her stockings muddy. (The Monkey Garden)

28. "Why did you leave me all alone? I waited my whole life. You're a liar. They all lied. All the books and magazines, everything that told it wrong." (Red Clowns)

29. "When you leave, you must remember always to come back for the others. A circle, understand? You will always be Esperanza. You will always be Mango Street. You can't erase what you know. You can't forget who you are. (The Three Sisters)

30. "No, Alicia says. Like it or not you are Mango Street, and one day you'll come back, too." (Alicia & I)

31. "They will not know I have gone away to come back. For the ones I left behind. For the ones who cannot out. (Mango Says Goodbye Sometimes)

LESSON FIFTEEN

Objectives
1. To extend the story by means of a project
2. To work cooperatively in a group

Activity #1
Allow students to choose one of the following projects. Give them the class period to complete it. If students need more time, you can assign the project as homework or add another day onto the unit plan.

PROJECT IDEAS

1. Draw a book jacket that summarizes the story.
2. Write a critique of the book.
3. Make a time line showing the important events from the story.
4. Make a diorama showing one of the scenes from the book.
5. Make puppets and write a puppet show to illustrate one scene from the story.
6. Write a radio or television commercial to advertise the book.
7. Design a poster to advertise the book.
8. Make a comic book version of the story to share with younger readers.
9. Make a mobile showing the main character, secondary characters and setting.
10. Create a poster describing a scene or a character.
11. Create a poster summarizing one of the chapters.
12. Make a collage based on scenes from the book.

WRITING ASSIGNMENT #3 - *House on Mango Street*

PROMPT

The House on Mango Street is autobiographical, although it is not a complete autobiography. Esperanza Cordero's experiences are based on the experiences and people that Sandra Cisneros knew as a child. She includes character descriptions of the important people in her life, vivid descriptions of the places she lived, and details about the events that occurred. Most importantly, she offers an insight into her own reactions, thoughts, and feelings.

Your assignment is to write a brief autobiographical sketch, about the length of one of the chapters in the novel.

PREWRITING

Ms. Cisneros includes many vignettes in The House on Mango Street. You should try to focus on one event or memory, much as Cisneros has done in her short chapters. It may help you to make a time line of the significant events in your life. Then you can choose what you want to write about.

You may want to interview people who knew you as a young child. You should prepare a list of questions ahead of time for them to answer, and also be ready to listen to them reminisce. You may want to tape record the interviews so that you can listen to them again as you are writing. It may also be helpful to look at old photographs. If you have moved, and if possible, visit the neighborhood where you used to live.

Organize the events in a chronological order so that the reader can follow the events as they occurred in your life.

DRAFTING

First, write a paragraph in which you introduce an important event in your life. Make sure you include background information about the setting (year, location) and the other people involved.

In the body of your autobiographical sketch, continue telling about the event or events, adding details about the other people involved. Make sure to include observations about your own thoughts and feelings.

Finally, write a concluding paragraph in which you talk about the ways that the event/events you wrote about have influenced your life today.

PEER EDITING/REVISING

When you finish the rough draft of your paper, ask another student to read it. After reading your rough draft, he/she should tell you what he/she liked best about your work, which parts were difficult to understand, and ways in which your work could be improved. Reread your paper considering your critic's comments, and make the corrections you think are necessary.

LESSON SIXTEEN

Objectives
  1. To compare predictions made at the beginning of the novel with actual events
  2. To complete all previous assignments

Activity #1

Use the rest of the class period to have students go through their notes and worksheets and check to see that all work has been completed.

Activity #2

If students have completed all assignments and there is extra class time, choose one of the Unit Review activities in Lesson 18 or 19 and do it now.

LESSON SEVENTEEN

Objectives
  1. To widen the breadth of students' knowledge about the topics discussed or touched upon in *The House on Mango Street*
  2. To check students' non-fiction assignments

Activity

Ask each student to give a brief oral report about the nonfiction work he/she read for the nonfiction assignment. Your criteria for evaluating this report will vary depending on the level of your students. You may wish for students to give a complete report without using notes of any kind, or you may want students to read directly from a written report, or you may want to do something in between these two extremes. Just make students aware of your criteria in ample time for them to prepare their reports.

Start with one student's report. After that, ask if anyone else in the class has read on a topic related to the first student's report. If no one has, choose another student at random. After each report, be sure to ask if anyone has a report related to the one just completed. That will help keep a continuity during the discussion of the reports.

Invite students to give positive feedback to the speakers. You may want to have students write a short note to the speaker after each presentation and pass the note to the speaker.

LESSON EIGHTEEN

Student Objective
To review all of the vocabulary work done in this unit

VOCABULARY REVIEW ACTIVITIES

1. Divide your class into two teams and have an old-fashioned spelling or definition bee.

2. Give individuals or groups of students a Vocabulary Word Search Puzzle. The person (group) to find all of the vocabulary words in the puzzle first wins.

3. Give students a Vocabulary Word Search Puzzle without the word list. The person or group to find the most vocabulary words in the puzzle wins.

4. Put a Vocabulary Crossword Puzzle onto a transparency on the overhead projector and do the puzzle together as a class.

5. Give students a Vocabulary Matching Worksheet to do.

6. Use words from the word jumble page and have students spell them correctly.

7. Play Vocabulary Bingo with the materials enclosed with this unit. The Caller calls out definitions for the vocabulary words. If a student has that word on his/her card, that word is covered with a piece of paper. When someone gets a column, row, or diagonal filled-in he/she yells out, "Bingo!" and wins that round.

8. Have students write a story in which they correctly use as many vocabulary words as possible. Have students read their compositions orally. Post the most original compositions on your bulletin board.

9. Have students work in teams and play charades with the vocabulary words.

10. Select a word of the day and encourage students to use it correctly in their writing and speaking vocabulary.

11. Have a contest to see which students can find the most vocabulary words used in other sources. You may want to have a bulletin board available so the students can write down their word, the sentence it was used in, and the source.

LESSON NINETEEN

Objective
   To review the main ideas presented in *The House on Mango Street*

Activity #1
   Choose one of the review games/activities included in the packet and spend your class period as outlined there.

Activity #2
   Remind students of the date for the Unit Test. Stress the review of the Study Guides and their class notes as a last minute, brush-up review for homework.

REVIEW GAMES / ACTIVITIES

1. Ask the class to make up a unit test for *The House on Mango Street*. The test should have 4 sections: multiple choice, true/false, short answer and essay. Students may use ½ period to make the test, including a separate answer sheet, and then swap papers and use the other ½ class period to take a test a classmate has devised.

2. Take ½ period for students to make up true and false questions (including the answers). Collect the papers and divide the class into two teams. Draw a big tic-tac-toe board on the chalk board. Make one team X and one team O. Ask questions to each side, giving each student one turn. If the question is answered correctly, that student's team's letter (X or O) is placed in the box. If the answer is incorrect, no mark is placed in the box. The object is to get three marks in a row like tic-tac-toe. You may want to keep track of the number of games won for each team.

3. Take ½ period for students to make up questions (true/false and short answer). Collect the questions. Divide the class into two teams. You'll alternate asking questions to individual members of teams A & B (like in a spelling bee). The question keeps going from A to B until it is correctly answered, then a new question is asked. A correct answer does not allow the team to get another question. Correct answers are +2 points; incorrect answers are -1 point.

4. Allow students time to quiz each other (in pairs) from their study guides and class notes.

5. Give students a crossword puzzle to complete.

6. Play bingo using the materials included with this unit. The Caller gives clues to which the students must know the one-word answer. If that answer appears on their cards, they place a piece of paper over that word. The first student to have a filled-in row, column or diagonal (like bingo) wins! (You should have students call off their filled-in words to make sure that all of their responses were correct).

Mango Street Review Games / Activities Continued

7. Divide your class into two teams. Use the crossword words with their letters jumbled as a word list. Student 1 from Team A faces off against Student 1 from Team B. You write the first jumbled word on the board. The first student (1A or 1B) to unscramble the word wins the chance for his/her team to score points. If 1A wins the jumble, go to student 2A and give him/her a clue. He/she must give you the correct word which matches that clue. If he/she does, Team A scores a point, and you give student 3A a clue for which you expect another correct response. Continue giving Team A clues until some team member makes an incorrect response. An incorrect response sends the game back to the jumbled-word face off, this time with students 2A and 2B. Instead of repeating giving clues to the first few students of each team, continue with the student after the one who gave the last incorrect response on the team.

8. Take on the persona of "The Answer Person." Allow students to ask any question about the book. Answer the questions, or tell students where to look in the book to find the answer.

9. Students may enjoy playing charades with events from the story. Select a student to start. Give him/her a card with a scene or event from the story. Allow the players to use their books to find the scene being described. The first person to guess each charade performs the next one.

10. Play a categories-type quiz game. (A master is included in this Unit Plan). Make an overhead transparency of the categories form. Divide the class into teams of three or four players each. Have each team Choose a recorder and a banker. Choose a team to go first. That team will choose a category and point amount. Ask the question to the entire class.(Use the Study Guide Quiz and Vocabulary questions.) Give the teams one minute to discuss the answer and write it down. Walk around the room and check the answers. Each team that answers correctly receives the points. (Incorrect answers are not penalized; they just don't receive any points). Cross out that square on the playing board. Play continues until all squares have been used. The winning team is the one with the most points. You can assign bonus points to any square or squares you choose.

11. Have individual students draw scenes from the book. Display the scenes and have the rest of the class look in their books to find the chapter or section that is being depicted. The first student to find the correct scene then displays his or her picture. When the game is over, collect the pictures and put them in a binder for students to look at during their free time.

NOTE: If students do not need the extra review, omit this lesson and go on to the test.

LESSON TWENTY

Objective
　　To demonstrate understanding of the vocabulary, main themes and events in *The House on Mango Street* by taking a test

Activity
　　Distribute copies of the test. Allow the entire class period for the test.

QUIZ GAME
House on Mango Street

1-8	9-10	11-13	14	15-16	17
100	100	100	100	100	100
200	200	200	200	200	200
300	300	300	300	300	300
400	400	400	400	400	400
500	500	500	500	500	500

UNIT TESTS

SHORT ANSWER UNIT TEST 1 - *House on Mango Street*

I. Matching

___ 1. Mango Street   A   made Esperanza feel stupid
___ 2. three sisters   B. only ones who understand Esperanza
___ 3. baby boy   C. Nenny's real name
___ 4. music box   D. Sally met the boys there; Esperanza wanted to run
___ 5. monkey garden   E. told Esperanza to return to Mango Street
___ 6. Mexican-American   F. name that Esperanza wants
___ 7. Magdalena   G. first house the family owned
___ 8. Puerto Rican   H. Marin's nationality
___ 9. Zeze the X   I. sang Pepsi commercials in English
___10. trees   J. Esperanza's nationality

II. Short Answer

1. Describe the house on Mango Street.

2. What is special about the tree in Meme's yard?

3. What matters, according to Marin?

4. What happened when Esperanza took the note asking if she could stay for lunch?

Mango Street Short Answer Unit Test 1 Page 2

5. What did the girls do to Aunt Lupe? Why did they do it? What happened to Aunt Lupe that day? What did Esperanza's mother say about it?

III. Fill in the Blanks

The House on Mango Street is the story of a young girl who grows up in a barrio neighborhood in Chicago. Before they moved to Mango Street, the (1) _____ family lived in a house on (2) _____ Street. They lived in several other places before that. Esperanza likes the house on Mango Street because the family (3) _____ the house for the first time.

Esperanza has two brothers and a younger sister named (4) _____. Her younger sister's real name is (5) _____. Esperanza is named for her (6) _____. She wishes she could change her name to something like (7) _____.

Throughout the book the reader gets a sense of what growing up as a (8) _____ American girl is like. Esperanza still wants to run and play when her friend, (9) _____ is meeting boys in the (10) _____.

Esperanza has her cards read by (11) _____, who tells her she will have a home in the heart. Then she meets the (12) _____, who reminds her to come back to Mango Street. In the end, she agrees that she must do this.

IV. Essay

    How did Esperanza change over the course of the novel? Were these changes for the better?

Mango Street Short Answer Unit Test 1 Page 4

V. Vocabulary

Listen to the vocabulary words and spell them. After you have spelled all the words, go back and write down definitions for them.

WORD	DEFINITION
1	
2	
3	
4	
5	
6	
7	
8	
9	
10	

Vocabulary Part 2 Matching

_____ 1. responsibility   A. heavy object used to keep something in place
_____ 2. anchor   B. done every year
_____ 3. goblets   C. duty
_____ 4. raven   D. rubber suction cups on sticks
_____ 5. currency   E. uncontrolled laughter or crying
_____ 6. annual   F. a sharp, vibrating sound
_____ 7. plungers   G. a large bird with black feathers
_____ 8. twangy   H. money
_____ 9. temporary   I. for a short time; not permanent
_____ 10. hysterical   J. glasses with stems and bases

ANSWER KEY: SHORT ANSWER UNIT TEST 1 - *House on Mango Street*

I. Matching

G	1. Mango Street	A	made Esperanza feel stupid
E	2. three sisters	B.	only ones who understand Esperanza
I	3. baby boy	C.	Nenny's real name
A	4. music box	D.	Sally met the boys there; Esperanza wanted to run
D	5. monkey garden	E.	told Esperanza to return to Mango Street
J	6. Mexican-American	F.	name that Esperanza wants
C	7. Magdalena	G.	first house the family owned
H	8. Puerto Rican	H.	Marin's nationality
E	9. Zeze the X	I.	sang Pepsi commercials in English
B	10. trees	J.	Esperanza's nationality

II. Short Answer

1. Describe the house on Mango Street.

    It is small and red, with small windows. Some of the bricks are crumbling. The front door is hard to open. There is no front yard. There is a small garage in the back. The house has stairs, but only one bedroom and one bathroom.

2. What is special about the tree in Meme's yard?

    The kids chose it for their First Annual Tarzan Jumping Contest. Although he won, Meme broke both arms during the contest.

3. What matters, according to Marin?

    It matters if the boys see them and they see the boys.

4. What happened when Esperanza took the note asking if she could stay for lunch?

    The nun said she could only stay that day. She cried in the canteen and ate her greasy, cold sandwich.

5. What did the girls do to Aunt Lupe? Why did they do it? What happened to Aunt Lupe that day? What did Esperanza's mother say about it?

    The girls pretended to be like Aunt Lupe. They mimicked her laugh, walk, and speech. She died the day they were making fun of her. Esperanza's mother said she was born on an evil day and would go to hell.

III. Fill in the Blanks

The House on Mango Street is the story of a young girl who grows up in a barrio neighborhood in Chicago. Before they moved to Mango Street, the (1) CORDERO family lived in a house on (2) LOOMIS Street. They lived in several other places before that. Esperanza likes the house on Mango Street because the family (3) OWNS the house for the first time.

Esperanza has two brothers and a younger sister named (4) NENNY. Her younger sister's real name is (5) MAGDALENA. Esperanza is named for her (6) GREAT-GRANDMOTHER. She wishes she could change her name to something like (7) ZEZE THE X.

Throughout the book the reader gets a sense of what growing up as a (8) MEXICAN-American girl is like. Esperanza still wants to run and play when her friend, (9) SALLY is meeting boys in the (10) MONKEY GARDEN.

Esperanza has her cards read by (11) ELENITA, who tells her she will have a home in the heart. Then she meets the (12) THREE SISTERS, who reminds her to come back to Mango Street. In the end, she agrees that she must do this.

IV. Essay

How did Esperanza change over the course of the novel? Were these changes for the better? Answers will depend on your class discussions.

V. Vocabulary   Choose ten of the vocabulary words to read orally for your class.

WORD	DEFINITION
1	
2	
3	
4	
5	
6	
7	
8	
9	
10	

Vocabulary Part 2 Matching

C   1. responsibility   A.   heavy object used to keep something in place
A   2. anchor   B.   done every year
J   3. goblets   C.   duty
G   4. raven   D.   rubber suction cups on sticks
H   5. currency   E.   uncontrolled laughter or crying
B   6. annual   F.   a sharp, vibrating sound
D   7. plungers   G.   a large bird with black feathers
F   8. twangy   H.   money
I   9. temporary   I.   for a short time; not permanent
E   10. hysterical   J.   glasses with stems and bases

SHORT ANSWER UNIT TEST 2 - *House on Mango Street*

I. Matching

____ 1. Earl   A. no one was sure what his wife looked like
____ 2. Darius   B. dances with Esperanza
____ 3. Great-Grandmother   C. has too many children
____ 4. Nenny   D. younger sister who is like Esperanza in many ways
____ 5. Loomis   E. Esperanza compares her hips to one
____ 6. Rosa Vargas   F. Esperanza doesn't want to grow up like her
____ 7. Rafaela   G. type of car Louie's cousin steals
____ 8. Cadillac   H. says a cloud is God
____ 9. Buick   I. drinks coconut and papaya juices
____ 10. Uncle Nacho   J. home between Mango and Keeler

II. Short Answer

1. What two things does Esperanza want to have someday?

2. What scares the people who come into Esperanza's neighborhood? What does Esperanza think of them?

3. What does Esperanza say about Alicia?

Mango Street Short Answer Unit Test 2 Page 2

4. What news had Papa received? How did he react? What did Esperanza do?

5. How does Esperanza feel about Mango Street?

III. Fill in the Blank

1. Ruthie doesn't _____.
2. _____ is the younger sister who thinks like Esperanza.
3. Cathy says _____.
4. Mr. Benny is _____.
5. The kids had a ride in _____.
6. A woman gave the girls some _____.
7. The music box makes Esperanza _____.
8. Louie's cousin Marin _____.
9. Esperanza chipped in to _____.
10. Esperanza wanted to eat lunch _____.
11. Geraldo _____.
12. Esperanza's great-grandmother used to _____.
13. Esperanza compares her _____ to a Buick.
14. Meme won _____.
15. Esperanza says she likes to _____.
16. Mamacita _____.

Mango Street Short Answer Unit Test 2 Page 3

IV. Essay   With what issues does the book deal? Does it do so in a realistic way? Explain in detail.

Mango Street Short Answer Unit Test 2 Page 4

V. Vocabulary

Listen to the vocabulary words and spell them. After you have spelled all the words, go back and write down the definitions.

WORD	DEFINITION
1	
2	
3	
4	
5	
6	
7	
8	
9	
10	

Vocabulary Part 2   Matching

_____ 1. ignition   A. done as if by machine
_____ 2. luxury   B. an entrance or doorway
_____ 3. automatically   C. weak; without much energy
_____ 4. strutted   D. the switch that turns on a car
_____ 5. threshold   E. to receive from one who has gone before
_____ 6. trudged   F. not easy to understand
_____ 7. anemic   G. satisfied
_____ 8. complicated   H. walked in a pompous way
_____ 9. inherit   I. comfort and pleasure
_____ 10. content   J. walked in a heavy-footed way; plodded

ANSWER KEY: SHORT ANSWER UNIT TEST 2 - *House on Mango Street*

I. Matching

A	1. Earl	A.	no one was sure what his wife looked like
H	2. Darius	B.	dances with Esperanza
F	3. Great-Grandmother	C.	has too many children
D	4. Nenny	D.	younger sister who is like Esperanza in many ways
J	5. Loomis	E.	Esperanza compares her hips to one
C	6. Rosa Vargas	F.	Esperanza doesn't want to grow up like her
I	7. Rafaela	G.	type of car Louie's cousin steals
G	8. Cadillac	H.	says a cloud is God
E	9. Buick	I.	drinks coconut and papaya juices
B	10. Uncle Nacho	J.	home between Mango and Keeler

II. Short Answer

1. What two things does Esperanza want to have someday?
    She wants to have a best friend and a house of her own.

2. What scares the people who come into Esperanza's neighborhood? What does Esperanza think of them?
    They think the residents are dangerous. Esperanza thinks they are stupid.

3. What does Esperanza say about Alicia?
    She is a good girl. She studies because she wants a better life. Alicia isn't afraid of anything except mice and her father.

4. What news had Papa received? How did he react? What did Esperanza do?
    His mother had died. He began to cry. Esperanza held him.

5. How does Esperanza feel about Mango Street?
    She says she doesn't belong. She never wants to come from Mango Street.

III. Fill in the Blank

1. Ruthie doesn't **go out much or do much of anything**.
2. **Nenny/Magdalena** is the younger sister who thinks like Esperanza.
3. Cathy says **the neighborhood is getting bad**.
4. Mr. Benny is **the owner of the grocery store**.
5. The kids had a ride in **a stolen Cadillac**.
6. A woman gave the girls some **high heels to play with**.
7. The music box makes Esperanza **feel stupid**.
8. Louie's cousin Marin **is going back to Puerto Rico - sells Avon - watches the children**.
9. Esperanza chipped in to **buy a bike**.
10. Esperanza wanted to eat lunch **in the school canteen**.
11. Geraldo **died in a hit and run accident**.
12. Esperanza's great-grandmother used to **ride a horse**.
13. Esperanza compares her **hips** to a Buick.
14. Meme won **the Tarzan contest and broke both arms**.
15. Esperanza says she likes to **tell stories**.
16. Mamacita **sits by the window and plays the Spanish radio station - cries when her baby boy sings the Pepsi commercial in English**.

IV. Essay   With what issues does the book deal? Does it do so in a realistic way? Explain in detail. Answers will depend on your class discussions.

V. Vocabulary   Choose ten words to read orally for this section of the test.

Vocabulary Part 2   Matching

D	1. ignition	A.	done as if by machine
I	2. luxury	B.	an entrance or doorway
A	3. automatically	C.	weak; without much energy
H	4. strutted	D.	the switch that turns on a car
B	5. threshold	E.	to receive from one who has gone before
J	6. trudged	F.	not easy to understand
C	7. anemic	G.	satisfied
F	8. complicated	H.	walked in a pompous way
E	9. inherit	I.	comfort and pleasure
G	10. content	J.	walked in a heavy-footed way; plodded

ADVANCED SHORT ANSWER UNIT TEST - *House on Mango Street*

I. Matching

____ 1. Earl   A. no one was sure what his wife looked like
____ 2. Darius   B. dances with Esperanza
____ 3. Great-Grandmother   C. has too many children
____ 4. Nenny   D. younger sister who is like Esperanza in many ways
____ 5. Loomis   E. Esperanza compares her hips to one
____ 6. Rosa Vargas   F. Esperanza doesn't want to grow up like her
____ 7. Rafaela   G. type of car Louie's cousin steals
____ 8. Cadillac   H. says a cloud is God
____ 9. Buick   I. drinks coconut and papaya juices
____ 10. Uncle Nacho   J. home between Mango and Keeler

II. Short Answer

1. What is the symbolism of the sweet drinks that Rafaela drinks?

2. What does Esperanza's comparison of herself to the trees say about her?

3. What social comment is Esperanza making in "Those Who Don't"?

4. What is Cisneros saying about women in general, and Hispanic women in particular?

5. How did Esperanza change over the course of the novel? Were these changes for the better?

Mango Street Advanced Short Answer Unit Test Page 2

III. Quotations   Discuss the meaning of the following quotations.

1. "For the time being, Mama says. Temporary, says Papa. But I know how these things go."

2. "I would like to baptize myself under a new name, a name more like the real me, the one nobody sees."

3. "One day you wake up and they are there. Ready and waiting like a new Buick with the keys in the ignition. Ready to take you where?"

4. "Who was it that said I was getting too old to play the games? Who was it I didn't listen to? I only remember that when the others ran, I wanted to run, too, up and down and through the monkey garden, fast as the boys, not like Sally who screamed if she got her stockings muddy."

5. "They will not know I have gone away to come back. For the ones I left behind. For the ones who cannot out."

Mango Street Advanced Short Answer Unit Test Page 3

IV. Vocabulary

Listen to the words and write them down. After you have written down all of the words, write a paragraph in which you use all of the words. The paragraph must in some way relate to *The House on Mango Street*.

1. _____
2. _____
3. _____
4. _____
5. _____

6. _____
7. _____
8. _____
9. _____
10. _____

MULTIPLE CHOICE TEST 1 - *The House on Mango Street*

I. <u>Matching/ Identify</u>

Directions: Place the letter of the matching definition on the blank line.

___	1. Mango Street	A.	made Esperanza feel stupid
___	2. three sisters	B.	only ones who understand Esperanza
___	3. baby boy	C.	Nenny's real name
___	4. music box	D.	Sally met the boys there; Esperanza wanted to run
___	5. monkey garden	E.	told Esperanza to return to Mango Street
___	6. Mexican-American	F.	name that Esperanza wants
___	7. Magdalena	G.	first house the family owned
___	8. Puerto Rican	H.	Marin's nationality
___	9. Zeze the X	I.	sang Pepsi commercials in English
___	10. trees	J.	Esperanza's nationality

II. <u>Multiple Choice</u>

1. How was the house on Mango street different than the other houses the family had lived in?
    - A   It was the largest house they had ever lived in.
    - B   The government was paying for it.
    - C   It was their own house.
    - D   It was the first two-story house they had lived in.

2. True or False: Esperanza says Nenny is her best friend.
    - A   True
    - B   False

3. What did Esperanza buy? How did she go about buying it?
    - A   She chipped in with sisters named Rachel and Lucy. They all bought a bike.
    - B   She and her sister bought a fancy doll house with furniture.
    - C   She bought makeup from a friend who sold Avon.
    - D   She and her brothers bought a new dress for their mother.

4. What did the girls discover in the furniture store that made Esperanza feel stupid?
    - A   It was a full-length mirror.
    - B   It was a book in Spanish, and she could not read it.
    - C   It was a music box.
    - D   It was a television. She had never seen one.

Multiple Choice Test 1 *The House on Mango Street*

5. What matters, according to Marin?
   - A   Having good skin and nice clothes matters.
   - B   Having lots of money matters.
   - C   It matters if the boys see them and they see the boys.
   - D   Being loved matters.

6. True or False: People who come into Esperanza's neighborhood think the residents are dangerous.
   - A   True
   - B   False

7. Why doesn't Esperanza want to dance?
   - A   Her mother said it is a sin and she is not allowed to dance.
   - B   She does not know how.
   - C   She is embarrassed because she is wearing her old saddle shoes with her new dress.
   - D   She thinks the others will make fun of her.

8. True or False: Aunt Lupe died the day the girls made fun of her.
   - A   True
   - B   False

9. Esperanza asked about a house. What was Elenita's response?
   - A   She said, "There's no place like home."
   - B   She said "Ah, yes, a home in the heart. I see a home in the heart."
   - C   She said," You will never feel at home anywhere."
   - D   She said, "Your family is your home."

10. True or False: Esperanza is proud of coming from Mango Street.
    - A   True
    - B   False

Multiple Choice Test 1 *The House on Mango Street*

III. Quotations
Directions: Match the two parts of each quotation.

___ 1. "Until then I am a red balloon, a balloon _____ .

___ 2. "I would like to baptize myself under a new name, a name _____

___ 3. "In the meantime they'll just have to _____ .

___ 4. "And I think if my own Papa died what I would do. _____ .

___ 5. "I don't know _____ .

___ 6. "No, Alicia says. _____ .

___ 7. "Why did you leave me all alone? _____ .

___ 8. "I have begun my own quiet war. _____ .

___ 9. "My father says when he came to this country he _____ .

___ 10. "They never saw the kitchenettes. They never knew _____ .

A. more like the real me, the one nobody sees."

B. I waited my whole life. You're a liar. They all lied. All the books and magazines, everything that told it wrong."

C. about the two-room flats and sleeping rooms he rented, the weekly money orders sent home, the currency exchange. How could they?"

D. I hold my Papa in my arms. I hold and hold and hold him."

E. Simple. Sure. I am one who leaves the table like a man, without putting back the chair or picking up the plate."

F. tied to an anchor."

G. ate hamandeggs for three months. Breakfast, lunch, and dinner. Hamandeggs. That was the only word he knew. He doesn't eat hamandeggs anymore."

H. Like it or not you are Mango Street, and one day you'll come back, too."

I. move a little farther north from Mango Street, a little farther away every time people like us keep moving in."

J. which way she'll go. There is nothing *I* can do."

Multiple Choice Test 1 *The House on Mango Street*

IV. <u>Vocabulary Part 1</u>
   Place the letter of the matching definition on the blank line.

___	1.	responsibility	A.	heavy object used to keep something in place
___	2.	anchor	B.	done every year
___	3.	goblets	C.	duty
___	4.	raven	D.	rubber suction cups on sticks
___	5.	currency	E.	uncontrolled laughter or crying
___	6.	annual	F.	a sharp, vibrating sound
___	7.	plungers	G.	a large bird with black feathers
___	8.	twangy	H.	money
___	9.	temporary	I.	for a short time; not permanent
___	10.	hysterical	J.	glasses with stems and bases

<u>Vocabulary Part 2</u>
   Circle the letter next to the word that matches the definition.

11. **tiny spots**
    a. flecks
    b. goblets
    c. marimbas
    d. plungers

12. **an upright cylinder for water**
    a. hydrant
    b. annual
    c. anchor
    d. slant

13. **a room directly above the roof**
    a. chandelier
    b. ignition
    c. attic
    d. flats

14. **done by machine**
    a. anemic
    b. automatically
    c. hysterical
    d. temporary

15. **walked in a heavy-footed manner**
    a. baptize
    b. strutted
    c. trudged
    d. descended

16. **an entrance or doorway**
    a. currency
    b. threshold
    c. bazaar
    d. inherit

17. **a doctor who operates**
    a. ferocious
    b. surgeon
    c. intern
    d. raven

18. **small, oval shaped containers**
    a. slats
    b. nimbus
    c. naphtha
    d. capsules

19. **a washable floor covering**
    a. luxury
    b. linoleum
    c. chandelier
    d. pillar

20. **store or theater passageways**
    a. chandelier
    b. ignition
    c. attic
    d. aisles

MULTIPLE CHOICE UNIT TEST 2 - *The House on Mango Street*

I. Matching
Directions: Place the letter of the matching definition on the blank line.

____ 1. Earl
____ 2. Darius
____ 3. great-grandmother
____ 4. Nenny
____ 5. Loomis
____ 6. Rosa Vargas
____ 7. Rafaela
____ 8. Cadillac
____ 9. Buick
____ 10. Uncle Nacho

A. no one was sure what his wife looked like
B. dances with Esperanza
C. has too many children
D. younger sister who is like Esperanza in many ways
E. Esperanza compares her hips to one
F. Esperanza doesn't want to grow up like her
G. type of car Louie's cousin steals
H. says a cloud is God
I. drinks coconut and papaya juices
J. home between Mango and Keeler

II. Multiple Choice

1. Name the members of the narrator's family. (The House on Mango Street)
    A   Mama, Papa, Abuela, Kiki, and the narrator.
    B   Mama, Papa, Carlos, Kiki, Nenny, and the narrator.
    C   Mama, Papa, Carlos, Mariana, Nenny, and the narrator.
    D   Mama, Uncle Lucho, Kiki, Nenny, and the narrator.

2. Which sentence does **not** describe the house on Mango Street?
    A   It is large and blue.
    B   Some of the bricks are crumbling.
    C   There is no front yard.
    D   There is one bedroom and one bathroom.

3. What does the narrator want to have someday? (Boys & Girls)
    A   She wants to have a husband and five children.
    B   She wants to have a bedroom of her own.
    C   She wants to have a best friend.
    D   She wants to have a college education.

4. How does Esperanza describe her feet? (Chanclas)
    A   She says they are big and heavy like plungers.
    B   She says they are small and dainty like Cinderella's.
    C   She says they are her best feature.
    D   She says they are ugly and look like banana boats.

Multiple Choice Unit Test 2 *The House on Mango Street*

5. Esperanza asked about a house. What was Elenita's response? (Elenita, Cards ...)
    A   She said, "There's no place like home."
    B   She said "Ah, yes, a home in the heart. I see a home in the heart."
    C   She said," You will never feel at home anywhere."
    D   She said, "Your family is your home."

6. What is different about Ruthie? (Edna's Ruthie)
    A   She cannot speak.
    B   She never leaves the house.
    C   She speaks five languages.
    D   She is the only adult who likes to play.

7. Who or what are the only ones that understand Esperanza? (Four Skinny Trees)
    A   the dogs
    B   the flowers
    C   the clouds
    D   the trees

8. Why doesn't Esperanza go out with her family on Sundays anymore? (Bums in the Attic)
    A   She has too much homework.
    B   She does not like the way her father drives.
    C   She is busy going out with her friends.
    D   She is ashamed of the way they stare out the window at things they can't have.

9. True or False: Esperanza thinks Sally got married to escape. (Linoleum Roses)
    A   True
    B   False

10. What does Esperanza say she likes to do? (Mango Says Goodbye ...)
    A   She likes to paint pictures.
    B   She likes to write songs.
    C   She likes to tell stories.
    D   She likes to watch television.

Multiple Choice Unit Test 2 *The House on Mango Street*

III. Quotations
Directions: Match the two parts of each quotation.

1. "But the house on Mango Street _____ .

2. "Nenny says: Yes, that's Mexico all right. _____ .

3. "Marin, under the streetlight, dancing by herself, is singing the same song somewhere. _____ .

4. "But after a while _____ .

5. "You can never _____ .

6. "Most likely I _____ .

7. "When I am too sad and too skinny to keep keeping, when I am a tiny thing against so many bricks, then it is _____ .

8. "Rats? they'll ask. _____ .

9. "Who was it that said I was getting too old to play the games? Who was it I didn't listen to? I only remember that _____ .

10. "They will not know _____ .

A. you get tired of being worried about kids who aren't even yours."

B. I look at trees. When there is nothing left to look at on this street. Four who grew despite concrete. Four who reach and do not forget to reach. Four whose only reason is to be and be."

C. Bums, I'll say, and I'll be happy."

D. is not the way they told it at all."

E. I have gone away to come back. For the ones I left behind. For the ones who cannot out."

F. will go to hell and most likely I deserve to be there."

G. have too much sky."

H. That's what I was thinking exactly."

I. when the others ran, I wanted to run too, up and down and through the monkey garden, fast as the boys, not like Sally who screamed if she got her stockings muddy.

J. I know. Is waiting for a car to stop, a star to fall, someone to change her life."

Multiple Choice Unit Test 2 *The House on Mango Street*

IV. Vocabulary
Directions: Match the word and its meaning.

___	1.	ignition	A.	done as if by machine
___	2.	luxury	B.	an entrance or doorway
___	3.	automatically	C.	weak; without much energy
___	4.	strutted	D.	the switch that turns on a car
___	5.	threshold	E.	to receive from one who has gone before
___	6.	trudged	F.	not easy to understand
___	7.	anemic	G.	satisfied
___	8.	complicated	H.	walked in a pompous way; swaggered
___	9.	inherit	I.	comfort and pleasure
___	10.	content	J.	walked in a heavy-footed way; plodded

Vocabulary Part 2
Directions: Circle the letter next to the word that matches the definition.

11. **a large bird with black feathers**
    a. cumulus
    b. raven
    c. ignition
    d. naphtha

12. **a room directly below the roof**
    a. chandelier
    b. ignition
    c. attic
    d. flats

13. **a small cafeteria or lunchroom**
    a. slant
    b. threshold
    c. canteen
    d. luxury

14. **a brownish colored soap**
    a. naphtha
    b. pillar
    c. slats
    d. inherit

15. **a sharp, vibrating sound**
    a. temporary
    b. twangy
    c. cumulus
    d. luxury

16. **removed with the fingers**
    a. plucked
    b. flecks
    c. marimbas
    d. complicated

17. **apartments all on one floor**
    a. attic
    b. aisles
    c. nimbus
    d. flats

18. **went down**
    a. pillar
    b. ferocious
    c. chandelier
    d. descended

19. **far apart in relationship**
    a. distant
    b. bazaar
    c. currency
    d. trudged

20. **xylophone like instrument**
    a. marimbas
    b. slats
    c. linoleum
    d. hysterical

ANSWER SHEET   Multiple Choice Unit Tests
The House on Mango Street

I. Matching
1.
2.
3.
4.
5.
6.
7.
8.
9.
10.

II. Multiple Choice
1. (A) (B) (C) (D)
2. (A) (B) (C) (D)
3. (A) (B) (C) (D)
4. (A) (B) (C) (D)
5. (A) (B) (C) (D)
6. (A) (B) (C) (D)
7. (A) (B) (C) (D)
8. (A) (B) (C) (D)
9. (A) (B) (C) (D)
10. (A) (B) (C) (D)

III. Quotations
1.
2.
3.
4.
5.
6.
7.
8.
9.
10.

IV. Vocabulary
1.
2.
3.
4.
5.
6.
7.
8.
9.
10.
11.
12.
13.
14.
15.
16.
17.
18.
19.
20.

ANSWER SHEET KEY   Multiple Choice Unit Test 1 *The House on Mango Street*

To make an overlay, make a copy of this page, cut out the columns next to the answers for the matching and vocabulary sections, and take a hole punch and punch out the empty ( ) for the multiple choice section.

I. Matching		III. Quotations		IV. Vocabulary	
1.	G	1.	F	1.	C
2.	E	2.	A	2.	A
3.	I	3.	I	3.	J
4.	A	4.	D	4.	G
5.	D	5.	J	5.	H
6.	J	6.	H	6.	B
7.	C	7.	B	7.	D
8.	H	8.	E	8.	F
9.	F	9.	G	9.	I
10.	B	10.	C	10.	E
				11.	A
				12.	A
				13.	C
				14.	B
				15.	C
				16.	B
				17.	B
				18.	D
				19.	B
				20.	D

II. Multiple Choice
1. (A) (B) ( ) (D)
2. (A) ( ) (C) (D)
3. ( ) (B) (C) (D)
4. (A) (B) ( ) (D)
5. (A) (B) ( ) (D)
6. ( ) (B) (C) (D)
7. (A) (B) ( ) (D)
8. ( ) (B) (C) (D)
9. (A) ( ) (C) (D)
10. (A) ( ) (C) (D)

ANSWER SHEET KEY   Multiple Choice Unit Test 2 *The House on Mango Street*

To make an overlay, make a copy of this page, cut out the columns next to the answers for the matching and vocabulary sections, and take a hole punch and punch out the empty ( ) for the multiple choice section.

I. Matching
1. A
2. H
3. F
4. D
5. J
6. C
7. I
8. G
9. E
10. B

II. Multiple Choice
1. (A) ( ) (C) (D)
2. ( ) (B) (C) (D)
3. (A) (B) ( ) (D)
4. ( ) (B) (C) (D)
5. (A) ( ) (C) (D)
6. (A) (B) (C) ( )
7. (A) (B) (C) ( )
8. (A) (B) (C) ( )
9. ( ) (B) (C) (D)
10. (A) (B) ( ) (D)

III. Quotations
1. D
2. H
3. J
4. A
5. G
6. F
7. B
8. C
9. I
10. E

IV. Vocabulary
1. D
2. I
3. A
4. H
5. B
6. J
7. C
8. F
9. E
10. G
11. B
12. C
13. C
14. A
15. B
16. A
17. D
18. D
19. A
20. A

UNIT RESOURCE MATERIALS

BULLETIN BOARD IDEAS - *House on Mango Street*

1. Save one corner of the board for the best of students' writing assignments.

2. Take one of the word search puzzles from the extra activities packet and with a marker copy it over in a large size on the bulletin board. Write the clue words to find to one side. Invite students prior to and after class to find the words and circle them on the bulletin board.

3. Write several of the most significant quotations from the book onto the board on brightly colored paper.

4. Make a bulletin board listing the vocabulary words for this unit. As you complete sections of the novel and discuss the vocabulary for each section, write the definitions on the bulletin board. (If your board is one students face frequently, it will help them learn the words.)

5. Collect pictures of the area mentioned in the book.

6. Make a display of pictures of book jackets and artwork from the various editions of *The House on Mango Street*.

7. Display articles about Sandra Cisneros and other Chicana/Chicano writers.

8. Have students design postcards depicting the settings of the book.

9. Create a "memory box" bulletin board of items mentioned in the novel.

10. Have students illustrate a quote from the novel. Display the illustrations and quotations on the bulletin board.

EXTRA ACTIVITIES - *House on Mango Street*

One of the difficulties in teaching a novel is that all students don't read at the same speed. One student who likes to read may take the book home and finish it in a day or two. Sometimes a few students finish the in-class assignments early. The problem, then, is finding suitable extra activities for students.

The best thing I've found is to keep a little library in the classroom. For this unit on *House on Mango Street*, you might check out from the school library other related books by Sandra Cisneros. There are also many other novels by ethnic or women writers that students would enjoy reading. Several journals have critiques of Cisneros' works. Some of the students may enjoy reading these and responding either in writing or in discussion groups. Encourage students to find critiques on web sites as well.

Your students who have reading difficulties, or speak English as a second language, may benefit from listening to all or part of the book on tape. Perhaps your above-average readers could take turns tape recording chapters of the book.

Other things you may keep on hand are puzzles. We have made some relating directly to *House on Mango Street* for you. Feel free to duplicate them.

Some students may like to draw. You might devise a contest or allow some extra-credit grade for students who draw characters or scenes from *Mango Street*. Note, too, that if the students do not want to keep their drawings you may pick up some extra bulletin board materials this way. If you have a contest and you supply the prize (a CD or something like that perhaps), you could, possibly, make the drawing itself a non-returnable entry fee.

The pages which follow contain games, puzzles and worksheets. The keys, when appropriate, immediately follow the puzzle or worksheet. There are two main groups of activities: one group for the unit; that is, generally relating to the text, and another group of activities related strictly to the vocabulary.

Directions for these games, puzzles and worksheets are self-explanatory. The object here is to provide you with extra materials you may use in any way you choose.

MORE ACTIVITIES - *House on Mango Street*

1. Pick a chapter or scene with a great deal of dialogue and have the students act it out on a stage. (Perhaps you could assign various scenes to different groups of students so more than one scene could be acted and more students could participate.)

2. Have students design a book cover (front and back and inside flaps).

3. Have students design a bulletin board (ready to be put up; not just sketched).

4. Invite a story teller to tell one or more stories related to *The House on Mango Street*.

5. Help students design and produce a talk show. Choose one of the story incidents as the topic. The host will interview the various characters. Students should make up the questions they want the host to ask the characters.

6. Have students work in pairs to create an interview with one of the characters. One student should be the interviewer and the other should be the interviewee. Students can work together to compose questions for the interviewer to ask. Each pair of students could present their interview to the class.

7. Invite students who have read other books by Sandra Cisneros to present book talks to the class.

8. Have students hold small group discussions related to topics in the book. Assign a recorder and a speaker for each group. Have the speaker from each group make a report to the class.

9. Cisneros brings up many issues regarding the role of women in her Mexican-American culture, as well as issues of racial prejudice. Invite volunteers to hold a panel discussion on one of these topics.

WORD SEARCH - *House on Mango Street*

All words in this list are associated with *The House on Mango Street*. The words are placed backwards, forward, diagonally, up and down. The included words are listed below the word search.

```
T M A N G O H C A N S A L L Y A L U P E
D R F N T L P Z S H I X R D N N H O B G
M A E W K O N J O C B A T D N E J V I T
X S R E J O H E I R E H E X E L N A G S
G I L I S M S L C A T H Y E N A D R Y Z
R S Y Q U I A A O X H L R K C D J G F N
A T Q F Z S N K R B N I R I L G V A T A
C E B C W T D M D O S X X B H A Y S V G
H R Y E E D A V E Y S E E A L M A R I N
E S M E N M J I R H M Z N L U T E E C S
L E N J A N H F O G E I E S X N Y I L J
M S J C C T Y D S Z L S I Y I B X E F C
G L I B U I C K Z U R C C M O N K E Y L
C T V R R W Z F A O P U X B W S B K S J
A L E A F A R P H C L Y O D L A R E G D
```

ALICIA	DARIUS	LOOMIS	MINERVA	SALLY
BENNY	DAVEY	LUCY	MONKEY	SHOES
BIKE	EARL	LUPE	MUSIC	SIRE
BOBO	EDNA	MAGDALENA	NACHO	SISTERS
BOY	GERALDO	MAMACITA	NENNY	TREES
BUICK	GIL	MANGO	PAULINA	VARGAS
CANTEEN	HORSE	MARIN	RACHEL	ZEZE
CATHY	KEELER	MEME	RAFAELA	
CORDERO	LOIS	MEXICAN	RUTHIE	

CROSSWORD - *House on Mango Street*

ACROSS
5 Esperanza's nationality; __-American
6 Tried to fly and dropped from the sky
7 Kids don't agree on what his wife looked like
8 Dies in a hit and run accident
10 Esperanza compares her hips to one
11 Says the neighborhood is getting bad
13 Tells fortunes with cards
14 Says a cloud was God
16 Sire's girlfriend
17 Died the day the girls made fun of her
18 Won the contest and broke both arms
20 She is afraid of mice
21 The little sister, born in Chicago
22 Kind of box that made Esperanza feel stupid
23 sings Pepsi commercials; the baby ___

DOWN
1 Esperanza chipped in to buy it
2 Sits by the window and plays the Spanish radio
3 Esperanza wants to eat there
4 Esperanza noticed him looking at her
5. Nenny's real name
7 Ruthie's mother
9 Owner of the used furniture store
11 Type of car Louie's cousin steals
12 Chinese year of Esperanza's birth
13 Likes to tell stories
14 His brother has a crooked eye
15 Louie's cousin who sells Avon
17 Home between Mango and Keeler
18 The family owns the house on this street
19 A woman gives some to the girls to play with; high-heeled ___

CROSSWORD - *House on Mango Street*

ACROSS
5 Esperanza's nationality; __-American
6 Tried to fly and dropped from the sky
7 Kids don't agree on what his wife looked like
8 Dies in a hit and run accident
10 Esperanza compares her hips to one
11 Says the neighborhood is getting bad
13 Tells fortunes with cards
14 Says a cloud was God
16 Sire's girlfriend
17 Died the day the girls made fun of her
18 Won the contest and broke both arms
20 She is afraid of mice
21 The little sister, born in Chicago
22 Kind of box that made Esperanza feel stupid
23 Sings Pepsi commercials; the baby ___

DOWN
1 Esperanza chipped in to buy it
2 Sits by the window and plays the Spanish radio
3 Esperanza wants to eat there
4 Esperanza noticed him looking at her
5. Nenny's real name
7 Ruthie's mother
9 Owner of the used furniture store
11 Type of car Louie's cousin steals
12 Chinese year of Esperanza's birth
13 Likes to tell stories
14 His brother has a crooked eye
15 Louie's cousin who sells Avon
17 Home between Mango and Keeler
18 The family owns the house on this street
19 A woman gives some to the girls to play with; high-heeled ___

MATCHING QUIZ/WORKSHEET 1 - House on Mango Street

___ 1. LOOMIS   A. Owner of the used furniture store
___ 2. CATHY   B. Says the neighborhood is getting bad
___ 3. LUPE   C. Chinese year of Esperanza's birth
___ 4. TREES   D. ____-American; Esperanza's nationality
___ 5. PAULINA   E. Esperanza noticed him looking at her
___ 6. CORDERO   F. Esperanza's last name
___ 7. LOIS   G. Kids don't agree on what his wife looks like
___ 8. MAMACITA   H. ____ Vargas; has too many children
___ 9. GIL   I. Home between Mango and Keeler
___10. SISTERS   J. Sire's girlfriend
___11. EARL   K. Three ____ told Esperanza to come back to Mango Street
___12. CANTEEN   L. ____ Box; made Esperanza feel stupid
___13. ROSA   M. Aunt ____; died the day the girls made fun of her
___14. RACHEL   N. The only ones who understand Esperanza
___15. HORSE   O. Younger sister to Esperanza
___16. MUSIC   P. Wants to love and love
___17. NENNY   Q. Sits by the window and plays the Spanish radio
___18. KEELER   R. The little sister, born in Chicago
___19. RAFAELA   S. Home street between Paulina and Loomis
___20. MONKEY   T. Likes to drink coconut and papaya juices
___21. SIRE   U. Esperanza wants to eat there
___22. MAGDALENA   V. ____ Garden; kids go there to play
___23. MEXICAN   W. Nenny's real name
___24. EDNA   X. Home before Keller
___25. SALLY   Y. Ruthie's mother

KEY: MATCHING QUIZ/WORKSHEET 1 - House on Mango Street

I - 1. LOOMIS		A. Owner of the used furniture store
B - 2. CATHY		B. Says the neighborhood is getting bad
M - 3. LUPE		C. Chinese year of Esperanza's birth
N - 4. TREES		D. ____-American; Esperanza's nationality
X - 5. PAULINA		E. Esperanza noticed him looking at her
F - 6. CORDERO		F. Esperanza's last name
J - 7. LOIS		G. Kids don't agree on what his wife looks like
Q - 8. MAMACITA		H. ____ Vargas; has too many children
A - 9. GIL		I. Home between Mango and Keeler
K - 10. SISTERS		J. Sire's girlfriend
G - 11. EARL		K. Three ____ told Esperanza to come back to Mango Street
U - 12. CANTEEN		L. ____ Box; made Esperanza feel stupid
H - 13. ROSA		M. Aunt ____; died the day the girls made fun of her
R - 14. RACHEL		N. The only ones who understand Esperanza
C - 15. HORSE		O. Younger sister to Esperanza
L - 16. MUSIC		P. Wants to love and love
O - 17. NENNY		Q. Sits by the window and plays the Spanish radio
S - 18. KEELER		R. The little sister, born in Chicago
T - 19. RAFAELA		S. Home street between Paulina and Loomis
V - 20. MONKEY		T. Likes to drink coconut and papaya juices
E - 21. SIRE		U. Esperanza wants to eat there
W - 22. MAGDALENA		V. ____ Garden; kids go there to play
D - 23. MEXICAN		W. Nenny's real name
Y - 24. EDNA		X. Home before Keller
P - 25. SALLY		Y. Ruthie's mother

MATCHING QUIZ/WORKSHEET 2 - House on Mango Street

___ 1. BENNY   A. Likes to tell stories

___ 2. RAFAELA   B. Adult who likes to play

___ 3. TREES   C. Esperanza wants to eat there

___ 4. DAVEY   D. Esperanza's last name

___ 5. MINERVA   E. Says a cloud was God

___ 6. VARGAS   F. Home between Mango and Keeler

___ 7. BIKE   G. Kids don't agree on what his wife looks like

___ 8. CORDERO   H. Sits by the window and plays the Spanish radio

___ 9. EARL   I. ____ Rican; Marin's nationality

___ 10. HEELS   J. Louie's cousin who sells Avon

___ 11. GERALDO   K. Esperanza noticed him looking at her

___ 12. GRANDMOTHER   L. Aunt ____; died the day the girls made fun of her

___ 13. RUTHIE   M. Likes to drink coconut and papaya juices

___ 14. NENNY   N. Dies in hit and run accident

___ 15. MARIN   O. Sire's girlfriend

___ 16. MEME   P. The only ones who understand Esperanza

___ 17. SIRE   Q. Writes poems at night

___ 18. LUPE   R. Younger sister to Esperanza

___ 19. LOOMIS   S. Great-____; Esperanza is named for her

___ 20. LOIS   T. Esperanza chipped in to buy it

___ 21. CANTEEN   U. Won the contest and broke both arms

___ 22. DARIUS   V. Angel ____; tried to fly and dropped from the sky

___ 23. ESPERANZA   W. Mr. ____; grocery store owner

___ 24. PUERTO   X. High ____; a woman gives some to the girls to play with

___ 25. MAMACITA   Y. His brother has a crooked eye

KEY: MATCHING QUIZ/WORKSHEET 2 - House on Mango Street

W 1. BENNY   A. Likes to tell stories

M 2. RAFAELA   B. Adult who likes to play

P 3. TREES   C. Esperanza wants to eat there

Y 4. DAVEY   D. Esperanza's last name

Q 5. MINERVA   E. Says a cloud was God

V 6. VARGAS   F. Home between Mango and Keeler

T 7. BIKE   G. Kids don't agree on what his wife looks like

D 8. CORDERO   H. Sits by the window and plays the Spanish radio

G 9. EARL   I. ____ Rican; Marin's nationality

X 10. HEELS   J. Louie's cousin who sells Avon

N 11. GERALDO   K. Esperanza noticed him looking at her

S 12. GRANDMOTHER   L. Aunt ____; died the day the girls made fun of her

B 13. RUTHIE   M. Likes to drink coconut and papaya juices

R 14. NENNY   N. Dies in hit and run accident

J 15. MARIN   O. Sire's girlfriend

U 16. MEME   P. The only ones who understand Esperanza

K 17. SIRE   Q. Writes poems at night

L 18. LUPE   R. Younger sister to Esperanza

F 19. LOOMIS   S. Great-____; Esperanza is named for her

O 20. LOIS   T. Esperanza chipped in to buy it

C 21. CANTEEN   U. Won the contest and broke both arms

E 22. DARIUS   V. Angel ____; tried to fly and dropped from the sky

A 23. ESPERANZA   W. Mr. ____; grocery store owner

I 24. PUERTO   X. High ____; a woman gives some to the girls to play with

H 25. MAMACITA   Y. His brother has a crooked eye

JUGGLE LETTER REVIEW GAME CLUE SHEET - House on Mango Street

1. REOSH = 1. _____
Chinese year of Esperanza's birth

2. OSAR = 2. _____
____ Vargas; has too many children

3. ELEKRE = 3. _____
Home street between Paulina and Loomis

4. MCTIMAAA = 4. _____
Sits by the window and plays the Spanish radio

5. CCAAILLD = 5. _____
Type of car Louie's cousin steals

6. OHGRNRAEMTD = 6. _____
Great-____; Esperanza is named for her

7. VARENIM = 7. _____
Writes poems at night

8. MYEKON = 8. _____
____ Garden; kids go there to play

9. SAAVGR = 9. _____
Angel ____ ; tried to fly and dropped from the sky

10. AETENCN =10. _____
Esperanza wants to eat there

11. YLCU =11. _____
The big sister, born in Texas

12. OOBB =12. _____
Ruthie's dog

13. YNENN =13. _____
Younger sister to Esperanza

14. IILCAA =14. _____
Is afraid of mice

15. AIDRUS =15. _____
Says a cloud was God

16. AEDN =16. _____
Ruthie's mother

17. ILG =17. _____
Owner of the used furniture store

18. IMXNECA =18. _____
____-American; Esperanza's nationality

19. ENBNY =19. _____
Mr. ____; grocery store owner

20. IKBE =20. _____
Esperanza chipped in to buy it

21. OILS =21. _____
Sire's girlfriend

22. ERAL =22. _____
Kids don't agree on what his wife looks like

23. EPUL =23. _____
Aunt ____; died the day the girls made fun of her

24. MMEE =24. _____
Won the contest and broke both arms

25. CHAERL =25. _____
The little sister, born in Chicago

26. SLHEE =26. _____
High ____; a woman gives some to the girls to play with

27. ILNEEAT =27. _____
Tells fortunes with cards

28. CMIUS =28. _____
____ Box; made Esperanza feel stupid

29. YBBA =29. _____
The ____ Boy; sings Pepsi commercials

30. OHANC =30. _____
Uncle ____; dances with Esperanza

31. UPROTE =31. _____
____ Rican; Marin's nationality

32. SSISTER =32. _____
Three ____ told Esperanza to come back to Mango Street

33. NOMAG =33. _____
The family owns the house here

34. UAIPANL	=34. _____
	Home before Keller

35. EDVYA	=35. _____
	His brother has a crooked eye

36. EERST	=36. _____
	The only ones who understand Esperanza

37. UBKIC	=37. _____
	Esperanza compares her hips to one

38. AMLGNAEDA	=38. _____
	Nenny's real name

39. ODCEROR	=39. _____
	Esperanza's last name

40. AREDGLO	=40. _____
	Dies in hit and run accident

41. RNAMI	=41. _____
	Louie's cousin who sells Avon

42. SERI	=42. _____
	Esperanza noticed him looking at her

43. TRHUEI	=43. _____
	Adult who likes to play

44. EZEZ	=44. _____
	____ The X; the name Esperanza wants

45. TCYAH	=45. _____
	Says the neighborhood is getting bad

46. AARFALE	=46. _____
	Likes to drink coconut and papaya juices

47. LSLAY	=47. _____
	Wants to love and love

48. RZEESNPAA	=48. _____
	Likes to tell stories

49. MSOIOL	=49. _____
	Home between Mango and Keeler

KEY: JUGGLE LETTER REVIEW GAME CLUE SHEET - House on Mango Street

1. REOSH = 1. HORSE
Chinese year of Esperanza's birth

2. OSAR = 2. ROSA
____ Vargas; has too many children

3. ELEKRE = 3. KEELER
Home street between Paulina and Loomis

4. MCTIMAAA = 4. MAMACITA
Sits by the window and plays the Spanish radio

5. CCAAILLD = 5. CADILLAC
Type of car Louie's cousin steals

6. OHGRNRAEMTD = 6. GRANDMOTHER
Great-____; Esperanza is named for her

7. VARENIM = 7. MINERVA
Writes poems at night

8. MYEKON = 8. MONKEY
____ Garden; kids go there to play

9. SAAVGR = 9. VARGAS
Angel ____ ; tried to fly and dropped from the sky

10. AETENCN =10. CANTEEN
Esperanza wants to eat there

11. YLCU =11. LUCY
The big sister, born in Texas

12. OOBB =12. BOBO
Ruthie's dog

13. YNENN =13. NENNY
Younger sister to Esperanza

14. IILCAA =14. ALICIA
Is afraid of mice

15. AIDRUS =15. DARIUS
Says a cloud was God

16. AEDN =16. EDNA
Ruthie's mother

17. ILG =17. GIL
   Owner of the used furniture store

18. IMXNECA =18. MEXICAN
   ____-American; Esperanza's nationality

19. ENBNY =19. BENNY
   Mr. ____; grocery store owner

20. IKBE =20. BIKE
   Esperanza chipped in to buy it

21. OILS =21. LOIS
   Sire's girlfriend

22. ERAL =22. EARL
   Kids don't agree on what his wife looks like

23. EPUL =23. LUPE
   Aunt ____; died the day the girls made fun of her

24. MMEE =24. MEME
   Won the contest and broke both arms

25. CHAERL =25. RACHEL
   The little sister, born in Chicago

26. SLHEE =26. HEELS
   High ____; a woman gives some to the girls to play with

27. ILNEEAT =27. ELENITA
   Tells fortunes with cards

28. CMIUS =28. MUSIC
   ____ Box; made Esperanza feel stupid

29. YBBA =29. BABY
   The ____ Boy; sings Pepsi commercials

30. OHANC =30. NACHO
   Uncle ____; dances with Esperanza

31. UPROTE =31. PUERTO
   ____ Rican; Marin's nationality

32. SSISTER =32. SISTERS
   Three ____ told Esperanza to come back to Mango Street

33. NOMAG =33. MANGO
   The family owns the house here

34. UAIPANL =34. PAULINA
Home before Keller

35. EDVYA =35. DAVEY
His brother has a crooked eye

36. EERST =36. TREES
The only ones who understand Esperanza

37. UBKIC =37. BUICK
Esperanza compares her hips to one

38. AMLGNAEDA =38. MAGDALENA
Nenny's real name

39. ODCEROR =39. CORDERO
Esperanza's last name

40. AREDGLO =40. GERALDO
Dies in hit and run accident

41. RNAMI =41. MARIN
Louie's cousin who sells Avon

42. SERI =42. SIRE
Esperanza noticed him looking at her

43. TRHUEI =43. RUTHIE
Adult who likes to play

44. EZEZ =44. ZEZE
____ The X; the name Esperanza wants

45. TCYAH =45. CATHY
Says the neighborhood is getting bad

46. AARFALE =46. RAFAELA
Likes to drink coconut and papaya juices

47. LSLAY =47. SALLY
Wants to love and love

48. RZEESNPAA =48. ESPERANZA
Likes to tell stories

49. MSOIOL =49. LOOMIS
Home between Mango and Keeler

VOCABULARY RESOURCE MATERIALS

VOCABULARY WORD SEARCH - *House on Mango Street*

```
G P I L L A R I Q L R S N C I T T A R T
F O M Z I Q W T N W H A F I V J W O N W
P C B A M N L N R T D H V M S T H S I A
C L C L R M O A M R E S Y E M C S T M N
K O U R E I S L A T S R S N N I U R B G
D K M C L T M S E F H E N A A N R U U Y
L X U P K W S B H U L G L D P H G T S R
O Y L N L E D Y A U M N U C H E E T N A
H L U R M I D G S S O U X O T R O E W A
S A S W S R C P T I M L U N H I N D I Z
E U M T A R A A T W L P R T A T L S V A
R N A N R C L I T Z C C Y E D X L K Q B
H N T Y G F N J D E S C E N D E D C N H
T A L D E G D U R T D F G T S K C E L F
B A P T I Z E C H A N D E L I E R G N X
```

AISLES	CHANDELIER	GOBLETS	NAPHTHA	STRUTTED
ANCHOR	COMPLICATED	HYDRANT	NIMBUS	SURGEON
ANEMIC	CONTENT	IGNITION	PILLAR	THRESHOLD
ANNUAL	CUMULUS	INHERIT	PLUCKED	TRUDGED
ATTIC	DESCENDED	INTERN	PLUNGERS	TWANGY
BAPTIZE	DISTANT	LINOLEUM	RAVEN	
BAZAAR	FLATS	LUXURY	SLANT	
CAPSULES	FLECKS	MARIMBAS	SLATS	

VOCABULARY CROSSWORD - *House on Mango Street*

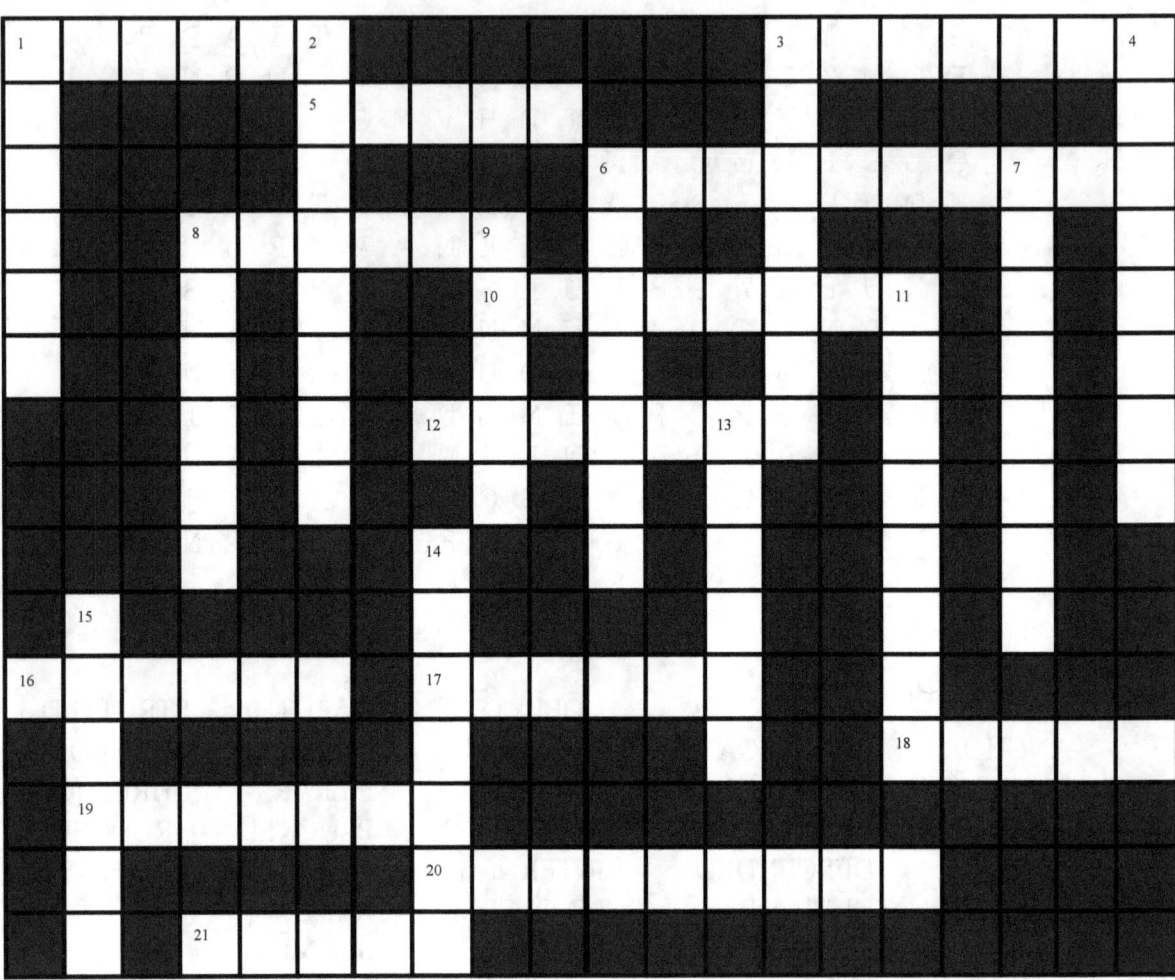

ACROSS
1. Weak; without much energy
3. White, fluffy clouds with a flat base
5. A room directly below the roof
6. A light fixture that hangs from a ceiling
8. Passageways in a store or theater
10. A washable floor covering
12. To receive from one who has gone before
16. A column or vertical support
17. A fair or sale
18. Narrow strips of wood or metal
19. To give a first or Christian name to
20. For a limited time
21. Apartments all on one floor

DOWN
1. Done every year
2. Small, oval shaped, jelly-like containers
3. Satisfied
4. Walked in a pompous way; swaggered
6. A small cafeteria or snack bar
7. The switch that turns on a car
8. Heavy object used to keep a boat in place
9. Slope; go in a diagonal direction
11. Wooden, xylophone-like instruments
13. An advanced student
14. Glasses with stems and bases
15. A low, dark rain cloud

VOCABULARY CROSSWORD ANSWER KEY - *House on Mango Street*

A	N	E	M	I	C					C	U	M	U	L	U	S
	N				A	T	T	I	C		O					T
	N			P					C	H	A	N	D	E	L	I	E	R
	U		A	I	S	L	E	S		A		T			G		U
	A		N	U		L	I	N	O	L	E	U	M		N		T
	L		C	L		A		T		N		A	I		I		T
			H	E		I	N	H	E	R	I	T		R	T		E
			O	S		T		E		N				I	I		D
			R			G		N		T				M	O		
	N					O				E				B	N		
P	I	L	L	A	R		B	A	Z	A	A	R		A			
	M							L				N		S	L	A	T	S
	B	A	P	T	I	Z	E										
	U						T	E	M	P	O	R	A	R	Y	
	S		F	L	A	T	S									

ACROSS
1 Weak; without much energy
3 White, fluffy clouds with a flat base
5 A room directly below the roof
6 A light fixture that hangs from a ceiling
8 Passageways in a store or theater
10 A washable floor covering
12 To receive from one who has gone before
16 A column or vertical support
17 A fair or sale
18 Narrow strips of wood or metal
19 To give a first or Christian name to
20 For a limited time
21 Apartments all on one floor

DOWN
1 Done every year
2 Small, oval shaped, jelly-like containers
3 Satisfied
4 Walked in a pompous way; swaggered
6 A small cafeteria or snack bar
7 The switch that turns on a car
8 Heavy object used to keep a boat in place
9 Slope; go in a diagonal direction
11 Wooden, xylophone-like instruments
13 An advanced student
14 Glasses with stems and bases
15 A low, dark rain cloud

VOCABULARY WORKSHEET 1 - House on Mango Stree

___ 1. PILLAR   A. Far apart in relationship
___ 2. BAZAAR   B. A column or vertical support
___ 3. CONTENT   C. Passageways in a store or theater
___ 4. FLATS   D. Slope; go in a diagonal direction
___ 5. AISLES   E. A fair or sale
___ 6. MARIMBAS   F. The switch that turns on a car
___ 7. CUMULUS   G. Satisfied
___ 8. CANTEEN   H. White, fluffy clouds with a flat base
___ 9. THRESHOLD   I. Small, oval shaped, jelly-like container
___ 10. PLUNGERS   J. Savage, fierce
___ 11. CURRENCY   K. For a limited time
___ 12. STRUTTED   L. A small cafeteria or snack bar
___ 13. ANCHOR   M. A low, dark rain cloud
___ 14. BAPTIZE   N. An entrance or doorway
___ 15. SLANT   O. Not easy to understand
___ 16. LUXURY   P. Comfort and pleasure
___ 17. COMPLICATED   Q. Rubber suction cups on sticks
___ 18. CAPSULES   R. Duty
___ 19. IGNITION   S. Heavy object used to keep a boat in place
___ 20. FEROCIOUS   T. To give a first or Christian name to
___ 21. DISTANT   U. Weak; without much energy
___ 22. TEMPORARY   V. Money
___ 23. ANEMIC   W. Wooden, xylophone-like instruments
___ 24. NIMBUS   X. Walked in a pompous way; swaggered
___ 25. RESPONSIBILITY   Y. Apartments all on one floor

KEY: VOCABULARY WORKSHEET 1 - House on Mango Stree

B - 1. PILLAR	A. Far apart in relationship
E - 2. BAZAAR	B. A column or vertical support
G - 3. CONTENT	C. Passageways in a store or theater
Y - 4. FLATS	D. Slope; go in a diagonal direction
C - 5. AISLES	E. A fair or sale
W 6. MARIMBAS	F. The switch that turns on a car
H - 7. CUMULUS	G. Satisfied
L - 8. CANTEEN	H. White, fluffy clouds with a flat base
N - 9. THRESHOLD	I. Small, oval shaped, jelly-like container
Q -10. PLUNGERS	J. Savage, fierce
V -11. CURRENCY	K. For a limited time
X -12. STRUTTED	L. A small cafeteria or snack bar
S -13. ANCHOR	M. A low, dark rain cloud
T -14. BAPTIZE	N. An entrance or doorway
D -15. SLANT	O. Not easy to understand
P -16. LUXURY	P. Comfort and pleasure
O -17. COMPLICATED	Q. Rubber suction cups on sticks
I - 18. CAPSULES	R. Duty
F -19. IGNITION	S. Heavy object used to keep a boat in place
J - 20. FEROCIOUS	T. To give a first or Christian name to
A -21. DISTANT	U. Weak; without much energy
K -22. TEMPORARY	V. Money
U -23. ANEMIC	W. Wooden, xylophone-like instruments
M 24. NIMBUS	X. Walked in a pompous way; swaggered
R -25. RESPONSIBILITY	Y. Apartments all on one floor

VOCABULARY WORKSHEET 2 - House on Mango Stree

___ 1. FLECKS   A. The switch that turns on a car
___ 2. FEROCIOUS   B. A washable floor covering
___ 3. PLUNGERS   C. A kind of soap
___ 4. CURRENCY   D. Weak; without much energy
___ 5. BAPTIZE   E. Heavy object used to keep a boat in place
___ 6. LINOLEUM   F. Uncontrolled laughing or crying
___ 7. CHANDELIER   G. Walked in a heavy-footed way; plodded
___ 8. PILLAR   H. To give a first or Christian name to
___ 9. DESCENDED   I. A column or vertical support
___10. TRUDGED   J. A light fixture that hangs from a ceiling
___11. ANEMIC   K. A sharp, vibrating sound
___12. IGNITION   L. Money
___13. INTERN   M. An advanced student
___14. CONTENT   N. Rubber suction cups on sticks
___15. HYDRANT   O. Apartments all on one floor
___16. NAPHTHA   P. Tiny spots
___17. FLATS   Q. Satisfied
___18. SURGEON   R. Went down
___19. ANCHOR   S. A doctor who operates on patients
___20. CUMULUS   T. White, fluffy clouds with a flat base
___21. HYSTERICAL   U. Small, oval shaped, jelly-like container
___22. AISLES   V. Passageways in a store or theater
___23. LUXURY   W. Savage, fierce
___24. CAPSULES   X. An upright cylinder for holding water
___25. TWANGY   Y. Comfort and pleasure

KEY: VOCABULARY WORKSHEET 2 - House on Mango Stree

P - 1. FLECKS		A. The switch that turns on a car
W - 2. FEROCIOUS		B. A washable floor covering
N - 3. PLUNGERS		C. A kind of soap
L - 4. CURRENCY		D. Weak; without much energy
H - 5. BAPTIZE		E. Heavy object used to keep a boat in place
B - 6. LINOLEUM		F. Uncontrolled laughing or crying
J - 7. CHANDELIER		G. Walked in a heavy-footed way; plodded
I - 8. PILLAR		H. To give a first or Christian name to
R - 9. DESCENDED		I. A column or vertical support
G - 10. TRUDGED		J. A light fixture that hangs from a ceiling
D - 11. ANEMIC		K. A sharp, vibrating sound
A - 12. IGNITION		L. Money
M - 13. INTERN		M. An advanced student
Q - 14. CONTENT		N. Rubber suction cups on sticks
X - 15. HYDRANT		O. Apartments all on one floor
C - 16. NAPHTHA		P. Tiny spots
O - 17. FLATS		Q. Satisfied
S - 18. SURGEON		R. Went down
E - 19. ANCHOR		S. A doctor who operates on patients
T - 20. CUMULUS		T. White, fluffy clouds with a flat base
F - 21. HYSTERICAL		U. Small, oval shaped, jelly-like container
V - 22. AISLES		V. Passageways in a store or theater
Y - 23. LUXURY		W. Savage, fierce
U - 24. CAPSULES		X. An upright cylinder for holding water
K - 25. TWANGY		Y. Comfort and pleasure

VOCABULARY JUGGLE LETTER REVIEW GAME CLUE SHEET - House on Mango Street

1. SRTDEHLOH = 1. _____
   An entrance or doorway

2. ASTSL = 2. _____
   Narrow strips of wood or metal

3. MNEIAC = 3. _____
   Weak; without much energy

4. CSUUUML = 4. _____
   White, fluffy clouds with a flat base

5. TATIC = 5. _____
   A room directly below the roof

6. RITNEN = 6. _____
   An advanced student

7. GRDDEUT = 7. _____
   Walked in a heavy-footed way; plodded

8. YRCCREUN = 8. _____
   Money

9. ABRMISAM = 9. _____
   Wooden, xylophone-like instruments

10. NAUNAL = 10. _____
    Done every year

11. LFSKEC = 11. _____
    Tiny spots

12. TGBELSO = 12. _____
    Glasses with stems and bases

13. SLEASCPU = 13. _____
    Small, oval shaped, jelly-like container

14. REUSGNO = 14. _____
    A doctor who operates on patients

15. EISASL = 15. _____
    Passageways in a store or theater

16. EVNRA = 16. _____
    A large bird with black feathers

17. NGPRUSEL =17. _____
Rubber suction cups on sticks

18. UMELOINL =18. _____
A washable floor covering

19. HETNIIR =19. _____
To receive from one who has gone before

20. NEDCDSEED =20. _____
Went down

21. EATENCN =21. _____
A small cafeteria or snack bar

22. TSDTNIA =22. _____
Far apart in relationship

23. ZPBTAIE =23. _____
To give a first or Christian name to

24. MTYOUAACTLILA =24. _____
Done by machine

25. TTDESRTU =25. _____
Walked in a pompous way; swaggered

26. OANRHC =26. _____
Heavy object used to keep a boat in place

27. ALTNS =27. _____
Slope; go in a diagonal direction

28. NNTIOIIG =28. _____
The switch that turns on a car

29. ALPIRL =29. _____
A column or vertical support

30. MRPETYARO =30. _____
For a limited time

31. ESPYOSLNIBIIRT =31. _____
Duty

32. ENTTCON =32. _____
Satisfied

33. URXLYU =33. _____
Comfort and pleasure

34. MEPOCLADCTI =34. _____
Not easy to understand

35. HAANTHP =35. _____
A kind of soap

36. YNADTRH =36. _____
An upright cylinder for holding water

37. WYATGN =37. _____
A sharp, vibrating sound

38. KCEUDPL =38. _____
Removed with the fingers

39. CTEYALHRSI =39. _____
Uncontrolled laughing or crying

40. RZAABA =40. _____
A fair or sale

41. ISMBUN =41. _____
A low, dark rain cloud

42. RSECIOOFU =42. _____
Savage, fierce

43. HIDLCNRAEE =43. _____
A light fixture that hangs from a ceiling

44. FSALT =44. _____
Apartments all on one floor

KEY: VOCABULARY JUGGLE LETTER REVIEW GAME CLUE SHEET - House on Mango Stree

1. SRTDEHLOH = 1. THRESHOLD
An entrance or doorway

2. ASTSL = 2. SLATS
Narrow strips of wood or metal

3. MNEIAC = 3. ANEMIC
Weak; without much energy

4. CSUUUML = 4. CUMULUS
White, fluffy clouds with a flat base

5. TATIC = 5. ATTIC
A room directly below the roof

6. RITNEN = 6. INTERN
An advanced student

7. GRDDEUT = 7. TRUDGED
Walked in a heavy-footed way; plodded

8. YRCCREUN = 8. CURRENCY
Money

9. ABRMISAM = 9. MARIMBAS
Wooden, xylophone-like instruments

10. NAUNAL =10. ANNUAL
Done every year

11. LFSKEC =11. FLECKS
Tiny spots

12. TGBELSO =12. GOBLETS
Glasses with stems and bases

13. SLEASCPU =13. CAPSULES
Small, oval shaped, jelly-like container

14. REUSGNO =14. SURGEON
A doctor who operates on patients

15. EISASL =15. AISLES
Passageways in a store or theater

16. EVNRA =16. RAVEN
A large bird with black feathers

17. NGPRUSEL	=17.	PLUNGERS
		Rubber suction cups on sticks
18. UMELOINL	=18.	LINOLEUM
		A washable floor covering
19. HETNIIR	=19.	INHERIT
		To receive from one who has gone before
20. NEDCDSEED	=20.	DESCENDED
		Went down
21. EATENCN	=21.	CANTEEN
		A small cafeteria or snack bar
22. TSDTNIA	=22.	DISTANT
		Far apart in relationship
23. ZPBTAIE	=23.	BAPTIZE
		To give a first or Christian name to
24. MTYOUAACTLILA	=24.	AUTOMATICALLY
		Done by machine
25. TTDESRTU	=25.	STRUTTED
		Walked in a pompous way; swaggered
26. OANRHC	=26.	ANCHOR
		Heavy object used to keep a boat in place
27. ALTNS	=27.	SLANT
		Slope; go in a diagonal direction
28. NNTIOIIG	=28.	IGNITION
		The switch that turns on a car
29. ALPIRL	=29.	PILLAR
		A column or vertical support
30. MRPETYARO	=30.	TEMPORARY
		For a limited time
31. ESPYOSLNIBIIRT	=31.	RESPONSIBILITY
		Duty
32. ENTTCON	=32.	CONTENT
		Satisfied
33. URXLYU	=33.	LUXURY
		Comfort and pleasure

34. MEPOCLADCTI =34. COMPLICATED
Not easy to understand

35. HAANTHP =35. NAPHTHA
A kind of soap

36. YNADTRH =36. HYDRANT
An upright cylinder for holding water

37. WYATGN =37. TWANGY
A sharp, vibrating sound

38. KCEUDPL =38. PLUCKED
Removed with the fingers

39. CTEYALHRSI =39. HYSTERICAL
Uncontrolled laughing or crying

40. RZAABA =40. BAZAAR
A fair or sale

41. ISMBUN =41. NIMBUS
A low, dark rain cloud

42. RSECIOOFU =42. FEROCIOUS
Savage, fierce

43. HIDLCNRAEE =43. CHANDELIER
A light fixture that hangs from a ceiling

44. FSALT =44. FLATS
Apartments all on one floor